T0114911

THE
FINAL
COUNTDOWN

THE COUNTDOWN TO THE
RETURN OF JESUS CHRIST HAS BEGUN

STEVE SPENCE

authorHOUSE®

AuthorHouse™
1663 Liberty Drive
Bloomington, IN 47403
www.authorhouse.com
Phone: 833-262-8899

Published by AuthorHouse 12/12/2023

ISBN: 979-8-8230-1870-8 (sc)
ISBN: 979-8-8230-1869-2 (e)

Library of Congress Control Number: 2023923378

Print information available on the last page.

BOOK ENDORSEMENTS

Steve Spence has compiled a succinct overview of the teachings of the Bible concerning the signs of the end of history as we know it. This book is clear and concise and easy to read. It is a great book to give to people in our world who are all desperately trying to make sense out of a society now spiralling into self-destruction.

The answers in this book also point people away from the global deception, which declares that man is capable of producing a better tomorrow, if we can all just work together under the control of a global elite.

Read this book more than once, and consider all the facts and bold predictions revealing a society out of control and desperately in need of hope.

The conclusion of this book is that there is a way of faith and hope, which can only be found in Jesus Christ, the Saviour of mankind.

Steve Penny – Snr Pastor Epic Church | Speaker | Author | Church Planter | Leadership Consultant | Founder of S4 GLOBAL

Pastor Steve Spence is a very successful pastor, teacher and mentor. His study of eschatology (end times) and growing awareness of critical world events combined with the lack of a clear "trumpet sound" coming from church leaders and Christians generally led to the writing of this book. It is a strong, well researched challenge for Christians to be aware of the perilous times ahead and glorious hope and certainty we have in our soon coming King. May you be challenged, stirred and inspired to know, understand and share the truths so clearly laid out in these pages.

Tim Hall – Evangelist | Tim Hall International Ministries

Final Countdown written by Pastor Steve Spence is a very clear prophetic picture of what is taking place and what is yet to take place in the coming days in our world. Steve's research into historical events is outstanding and he has spent many years preparing this book.

Having known Pastor Steve Spence for around forty years he is the most authentic person and a man of great character and trust. In a day when some church leaders are unsure or even fearful to expand on world events, Steve Spence is not. This book will certainly open your eyes and will help you draw closer to Jesus Christ in your personal life.

Mark Horan – Pastor | Coach | Mentor

CONTENTS

INTRODUCTION

It was 1962 when, as a twelve year old I was sitting at home with my mum and dad watching a news item on television reporting on the Cuban missile crisis. It was the height of the cold war and Russia was attempting to place ballistic missiles in Cuba. Naturally, this was seen by the Americans as a real threat to their security, so President John F Kennedy ordered a naval blockade of Cuba in order to stop the Russian ships from delivering their cargo of missiles, and the launching apparatus to fire them.

As we watched this unfolding on television, I clearly remember my mum being greatly concerned that we were on the brink of WW3, and her quoting a passage of scripture where the Bible speaks of the generation that sees Israel return as a nation to Palestine will see the end of the world. Now that isn't exactly what the Bible says, but mum was close to the mark when she said what she said, anyway more on that later.

Fast forward 15 years, my wife and I had just become Christians. We were so excited about our new-found faith that we started attending just about every Christian gathering we could. One of these meetings was a midweek Bible study group. While attending this meeting I heard once again that same thought being shared that my mum had spoken of all those years earlier. "The generation that sees Israel return as a nation..." However, this time the person speaking said, "Will see the second coming of Christ." Hearing that and remembering the words of my mother years earlier launched me into a long and detailed study of the Bible and what it had to say about the last days and Jesus return. In fact, I spent so much time studying end times I realised one day that I knew more about the coming Jesus than I knew about the Jesus who had come. I'm glad to say that after several years the Lord brought a balance back into my life, and revealed to me the surpassing value of knowing, in ever increasing ways, the Jesus who came into this world 2000 years ago. The most wonderful life changing thing a person can do is to know the Jesus who has come, and make Him Lord and Saviour of their life. However, I have also found the more I've discovered and learnt about Jesus' soon return to this planet the more inspired and motivated I am to live for Him, and to bring others to know the saving grace of the soon coming King as well. My prayer is that as you read through the pages of this book you too will be more motivated than ever to share the good news with others. I believe that understanding the times we're living in will inspire us to live for Him more than just about anything else.

CHAPTER 1

KNOWING THE SEASON

How many times have we heard people say that no one can fully understand what the Bible is really saying? That may be true in some instances, but there's also a great deal in the Bible that is very easy to understand. For example, the Bible is very clear about the fact that Jesus came into this world in human form. He lived a sinless life. He was crucified for our sins. He was buried and then He rose again defeating sin and death. He ascended into heaven, and He will return again to this planet. Jesus second coming is spoken of over and over again throughout the Bible. See Appendix (001) for just some of these references.

The Bible is so clear about Jesus coming back to this planet, and yet when I talk to people about this it seems they want to sidestep the topic altogether. Even among churches and church leaders the return of Christ is treated almost like a fairy-tale by some, or something that is so far out there in the future it's not worth considering or teaching on. It's obvious that not everyone is excited about the Lord's return. For example, some young singles are not too keen to hear about Jesus coming again, perhaps because they've got their plans for future adventures, travel, or they want to be married and have children. Then you have the young married who are starting a family and wanting to see their children grow up, they don't want to think about Jesus' return and the end of the world as we know it. What about the businessman just starting to see his business take off, he'd rather Jesus hang back awhile till he makes his millions. Also, the thought of Jesus returning to earth in our lifetime can be unsettling, even frightening to many people. An example of that is in *Acts 24:25* where Governor Felix became frightened after the Apostle Paul spoke to him about the coming day of judgement. The thought of judgement and the end of the world is something Felix didn't want to think about.

It is easy to understand why many people are quick to embrace the ideas put forward by some to promote the thinking that Jesus may not be coming back for thousands of years, if at all. For example, people can be quick to say, "Nothing has changed, we've always had Anti-Christ figures like Hitler, Idi Amin, and Stalin etc. We've always had earthquakes and wars and rumours of wars. Nothing has changed." But that is not what the Bible teaches. Consider the words of Peter in…

2 Peter 3:3–4 First, I want to remind you that in the last days there will come scoffers who will do every wrong they can think of and laugh at the truth. This will be their line of argument: "So Jesus promised to come back, did he? Then where is he?

He'll never come! Why, as far back as anyone can remember, everything has remained exactly as it was since the first day of creation." TLB

How many times have we heard that argument before? Well, the Bible says that kind of thinking comes from scoffers and mockers. The reality is, things have not always been the way they are now, and you'll see that as you read through the following pages.

Another line of thinking that stops people from giving serious consideration to Jesus' return is "no one knows when He is coming, so why think about it." Now there's an element of truth in that but it's not fully true. Let's take a close look at several scriptures.

1 Thessalonians 5:1-6 Now concerning how and when all this will happen, dear brothers and sisters, we don't really need to write you. For you know quite well that the day of the Lord's return will come unexpectedly, like a thief in the night. When people are saying, "Everything is peaceful and secure," then disaster will fall on them as suddenly as a pregnant woman's labour pains begin. And there will be no escape. But <u>you aren't in the dark about these things</u>, dear brothers and sisters, and you <u>won't be surprised</u> when the day of the Lord comes like a thief. For you are all children of the light and of the day; we don't belong to darkness and night. So be on your guard, not asleep like the others. Stay alert and be clearheaded. NLT

Paul is writing here to the church in Thessalonica, to believers, to children of the light and of the day, to those who are not in the dark, or blind to the times regarding

Jesus' return. Note, Paul clearly states that the believers will not be taken by surprise at the timing of His return.

Luke 21:34 "Be on guard, so that your hearts will not be weighted down with dissipation and drunkenness and the worries of life, and that day will not come on you suddenly like a trap. NASB

Revelation 3:3 'So remember what you have received and heard; and keep it, and repent. Therefore if you do not wake up, I will come like a thief, and you will not know at what hour I will come to you. NASB

The inference given in these two scriptures is that if we do remember, if we do obey, if we do stay on the alert, if we do wake up, the Lord's return will not come upon us as like a thief in the night, but rather we will know the time of His coming. Now I hasten to add that Jesus said, no man knows the day or the hour of His return. (*Matthew 24:36*) However, when Jesus said this, He was literally speaking of a 24 hour day and a 60 minute hour, and He was, I believe, referring to the rapture of the church. Now the aim of this book is not to teach on the rapture. However, it is important to understand the Bible teaches Jesus will return twice. Firstly, He will return for His Bride the church, He will come in the clouds and receive to Himself those who belong to Him. (*1 Thessalonians 4:17*) No one will know the day or the hour of this 'taking up' of the church. Some believe the rapture will take place at some time prior to what is known as The Great Tribulation. Others believe it will be at some time during the tribulation period, but as to the exact timing of this event no one knows, only God in heaven knows this. (*Matthew 24:36*)

Following the rapture, the Bible teaches that the Man of Lawlessness, otherwise known as the Anti-Christ will be revealed, (*2 Thessalonians 2:3,6-7*) he will usher in such gross evils and horrors that the world has never seen. After this, and after all that God has ordained to take place on earth, Jesus will return to bring to an end the evil, pain and suffering that Satan and his subordinates have brought against humanity. And it is at this time Jesus will establish His kingdom of righteousness on the earth once and for all. (*Revelation Ch19 Ch20*)

It is clear we won't know the day or the hour of the rapture, but as you read through the following pages you will find the Bible does teach we will know the season, or the generation Jesus is coming back to.

CHAPTER 2

Looking for Signs

One of the great discourses Jesus gave regarding His return is found in Matthew Chapter 24. It begins with Jesus' disciples asking a very clear question about the timing of His return and the signs to look for that would indicate His coming is near.

Matthew 24:1-3 As Jesus was leaving the Temple grounds, His disciples pointed out to Him the various Temple buildings. But He responded, "Do you see all these buildings? I tell you the truth, they will be completely demolished. Not one stone will be left on top of another!" Later, Jesus sat on the Mount of Olives. His disciples came to Him privately and said, "Tell us, when will all this happen? What sign will signal Your return and the end of the world?" NLT

Now it's worth noting that Jesus didn't say "I'm not going to tell you, there aren't any signs" no, He answered their question, "You want to know when I'm coming back to planet earth, well I'll give you some signs to look for." He went on to say in...

Matthew 24:33-34 "So also when you see these signs, all taken together, coming to pass, you may know of a surety that He is near, at the very doors. Truly I tell you, this <u>generation the whole multitude of people living at the same time, in a definite, given period</u> will not pass away till all these things taken together take place." AMPC

Jesus said we will not know the day or hour, but He does say there will be a generation of people, that if looking for the signs, will at the very least know the season in which He is coming. Now when Jesus spoke here of 'all these things' taking place in a generation and a given period of time. An often asked question is, "Over how many years is a generation?" There are varying opinions on this, some say when the Bible speaks of a generation it's speaking of 40 years, others say 70 years and others suggest 120 years. Regardless of how we define a generation Jesus is saying there will be people living at the same time, in a definite, given period that will see all the signs of His return coming together in their lifetime.

The reason we are given the signs, is because Jesus doesn't want His people ignorant of the timing of His return. The following scriptures make it abundantly clear that Jesus wants us to be alert and awake to the signs He's given us, and to what's happening in the world around us.

Luke 21:34-36 "<u>Watch out</u>...don't let that day catch you unaware, as in a trap. For that day will come upon everyone living on the earth. <u>Keep a constant watch</u>. NLT

Mark 13:33 And since you don't know when that time will come, <u>be on guard</u>! <u>Stay alert</u>…<u>Watch for His return</u>. NLT

Mark 13:35 You, too, <u>must keep watch</u>! For you don't know when the master of the household will return… NLT

Mark 13:37 "What I say to you I say to everyone: <u>Watch for his return</u>!" NLT

1 Thessalonians 5:6 …So <u>be on your guard</u>, <u>not asleep</u> like the others. <u>Stay alert</u> and <u>be clearheaded</u>. NLT

Rev 16:15 "<u>Keep watch</u>! I come unannounced, like a thief… MSG

Jesus wants His people aware of, and discerning the signs of the times; In fact, He actually rebukes those who don't keep watch and discern the times they are living in. Jesus, speaking to religious leaders, said in…

Matthew 16:2-3 "You know the saying, 'red sky at night means fair weather tomorrow, red sky in the morning means foul weather all day.' You are good at reading the weather signs in the sky, but <u>you can't read the obvious signs of the times</u>! NLT

On the other hand, He commends those who are looking for His coming.

1 Thessalonians 1:2-3 As we talk to our God and Father about you, we think of your faithful work, your loving deeds, and <u>your continual anticipation of the return of our Lord Jesus Christ</u>. NLT

The Bible is clear, the Lord wants us to be aware and awake regarding His return, and also to stay alert and be looking for signs or events that could reveal to us just how near His coming is.

We also need to remember the words of Jesus in *Matthew 24:33-34* that one specific generation of people living at a certain time in history will see, if their eyes are open, the signs the Bible speaks of, coming to pass in their lifetime. And when these signs become evident that generation should be expecting to see the coming of the Lord.

So, here's the question, are we seeing those signs today? Are we the generation Jesus was speaking of? What are the things happening at this time in history that we should be seeing if Jesus' coming is imminent? Let's consider what I believe to be 'signs' that clearly indicate His coming could be closer than you think.

CHAPTER 3

A NATION IN A DAY

I said earlier my mother made a statement regarding the nation of Israel returning to Palestine, and hearing a preacher say, "The generation that sees Israel return to Palestine as a nation will see the coming of Christ" Both my mum and the preacher were obviously referring to the words of Jesus in *Luke Chapter 21*. In my mind, this prophecy spoken by Jesus, is one of the most powerful, most significant prophecies given in scripture regarding the timing of the Lord's return. Jesus is speaking here of the events that would take place over the next two thousand plus years. When you look closely at what Jesus is saying in *Luke Chapter 21* you'll see He is speaking not just of one generation but the generations from 70AD through to this present time.

Luke 21:20 "But when you see Jerusalem surrounded by armies, then recognize that her desolation is near. 21 Then those who are in Judea must flee to the mountains, and those who are in the midst of the city must leave, and those who are in the country must not enter the city; 22 because these are days of vengeance, so that all things which are written will be fulfilled. 23 Woe to those who are pregnant and to those who are nursing babies in those days; for there will be great distress upon the land and wrath to this people; 24 and they will fall by the edge of the sword, and will be led captive into all the nations... NASB   Let's stop here for a moment.

History records that Jerusalem was besieged by Roman armies in 70AD. So approximately 40 years before that took place, Jesus prophesied a warning to the inhabitants of Jerusalem that when they saw those armies surrounding the city, they should not hang around but get out and away as far as they could. The Romans did overrun the city and many of those who did not flee were slaughtered, the remainder were, as Jesus said, led captive into all the nations. Then Jesus continued to prophesy...

"And Jerusalem will be trampled on by the Gentiles until the times of the Gentiles are fulfilled." NASB   The New Century Version of the Bible puts it this way, *"Jerusalem will be crushed by non-Jewish people until their time is over." NCV*

As always Jesus was right, for the next two thousand years Jerusalem was ruled over or trodden under foot by non-Jewish nations such as the Romans, Persians, Crimean Tartars, Crusaders, Egyptians, Syrians, Greeks, Mongolians, Germans, Turks, British, and Arabs. Until in 1948 the Jews returned to Palestine and on the 14th May became again the nation of Israel. Then in 1967 during what was known as the "Six Day War" they once again took control of the old city of Jerusalem.

For the first time since 70AD Jerusalem was back under Jewish control. The time of the Gentiles occupation of Jerusalem was over. Jesus said, "The generation that sees this will not pass away until all things take place" including His return. Is it any wonder my mother was so concerned about the Cuban missile crisis escalating into WW3?

It's time to turn to Jesus, repent of your sin, and invite Him to be your Saviour and the Lord of your life.

CHAPTER 4

Israel Prospering

When Israel returned to Palestine in 1948 the landscape wasn't much more than a desert. But through incredibly hard work, determination and the favour of God the infant nation began to blossom. Jesus prophesied this would be yet another sign to be looking for.

Matthew 24:32–34 From the fig tree learn this lesson: as soon as its young shoots become soft and tender and it puts out its leaves, you know of a surety that summer is near. So also when you see these signs, all taken together, coming to pass, you may know of a surety that He is near, at the very doors." AMPC

Throughout scripture the "Fig Tree" is symbolic for Israel. For example we see in…

Hosea 9:10 The LORD says, "O Israel, when I first found you, it was like finding fresh grapes in the desert. When I saw your ancestors, it was like seeing the first ripe figs of the season. NLT

Jeremiah 24:5-7 ‹Thus says the LORD God of Israel, ‹Like these good figs, so I will regard as good the captives of Judah, whom I have sent out of this place into the land of the Chaldeans. 'For I will set My eyes on them for good, and I will bring them again to this land; and I will build them up and not overthrow them, and I will plant them and not pluck them up. 'I will give them a heart to know Me, for I am the LORD; and they will be My people, and I will be their God, for they will return to Me with their whole heart. NASB

Jesus is saying, when you see the fig tree (Israel) blossoming and producing fruit, His coming is very near. Now throughout the previous two thousand years, the Jewish nation had not blossomed, in fact they were a very dead dry branch scattered like dust across the nations. But, it's in this generation, not hundreds of years back in the past, or sometime in the far distant future, but in this generation that Israel has come to life again. Israel has now become one of the wealthiest nations on earth for the size of its population and land mass.

At the time of writing Israel had the second-largest number of start-up companies in the world after the United States, (002) and the third largest number of NASDAQ listed companies after the United States and China. (003) It is the most developed and advanced country in western Asia (004) and the highest average wealth per adult in the Middle East. (005) In recent years Israel has had among the highest GDP growth rates within the developed world. (006)

Hosea prophesied that it would become an oasis in the desert and it has become that, not hundreds of years in the past and not at some time in the far distant future, but in this Generation. Jesus said when we see that sign, He is right at the door.

It's time to turn to Jesus, repent of your sin, and invite Him to be your Saviour and the Lord of your life.

CHAPTER 5

DECEPTION AND LIES

Jesus was asked by His disciples "What will be the sign of your coming and the end of the world?" (*Matthew 24:3*) In the very next verse He answered and gave them the first sign to be looking out for, which was deception.

Matthew 24:4 ...Be careful that no one <u>misleads</u> you, <u>deceiving</u> you and <u>leading you into error</u>. AMPC

Jesus is specifically speaking here about being led away from biblical truth, and being drawn or seduced away from God's ways into error through deception. The generation that sees His return will see a level of deception and lies such as the world has never seen before. It would be difficult to argue against the thought that we are seeing this today. I think it would be true to say, there has never been a time in history where the entire world is being led away from the truth of the gospel, and Christian values like in this generation.

The Bible reveals that the overall orchestrator of evil on the earth is the devil, and deception is his chief tool. He has always been the great deceiver. In *Genesis 3:1-5* we see the devil deceiving Eve, in *Revelation 20:3* we see the devil deceiving nations. He was a deceiver in the beginning and he'll be a deceiver to the end. Deceiving is what the devil does best. One of the names the Bible gives to the devil is the <u>Deceiver</u>.

Revelation 12:9 …That ancient serpent, who is called the devil and Satan, the <u>deceiver</u> of the whole world. ESV

The devil is deceiving the nations by working through people, in the same way God works through people. God works through His people (the church) to outwork His plans, and to have the truth of the Gospel proclaimed in the world. Likewise, the devil uses people to outwork his plans. He works through the global elite, through governments and the media, through corporations, organisations and individuals to outwork his plans of robbing, killing and destroying all that is holy, righteous and good. And he is using his weapons of deception and lies, to lead people away from God, to their destruction.

Matthew 24:24 For false Christs and false prophets will arise, and they will show great signs and wonders so as to deceive and lead astray, if possible, <u>even the elect</u>. AMPC

Never before have we seen the number of false Christs and false prophets raising their voices promoting lifestyles and values that are totally opposed to the truth of the Gospel. Remember the devil works through and speaks through people to outwork his evil schemes and lies to deceive the nations. For example…

- The deceivers and the deceived are saying, "Our planet and all life on it began with a big bang and it has evolved to where we are today." God is saying, "In the beginning I created the heavens and the earth and all that's within them."

- The deceivers and the deceived are saying, "Freedom will come if you follow the governments directions and rules." God is saying, "Freedom comes if you confess your sins and follow Jesus Christ."

- The deceivers and the deceived are saying, "listen to the experts advice and you'll be safe and secure." God is saying, "listen to the Holy Spirit's advice and you'll be safe and secure."

- The deceivers and the deceived are saying, "You can choose your gender." God is saying, "Male and female I made them."

- The deceivers and the deceived are saying, "Abortion is just removing an inconvenience." God is saying, "Abortion is murdering a Human Being."

- The deceivers and the deceived are saying, "You have the right to choose when you die. God is saying, "I number your days."

- The deceivers and the deceived are saying—Same sex marriage is to be applauded." God is saying, "A man shall leave his father and mother and marry a woman."

- The deceivers and the deceived are saying, "The way to global peace and prosperity is a one world government." God is saying, "The way to peace and prosperity is when the government is resting on My shoulders."

- The deceivers and the deceived are saying, "Climate change will destroy the earth." God is saying, "As long as the earth exists, planting and harvesting, cold and heat, summer and winter, day and night will never stop."

- The deceivers and the deceived are saying, "The Bible is full of hate speech." God is saying, "All scripture is inspired by God and is profitable for teaching, for correcting and for training in righteousness."

- The deceivers and the deceived are saying, "You can find your own truth." God is saying, "Jesus Christ is the Truth."

- The deceivers and the deceived are saying, "We're on the verge of a fourth industrial revolution." God is saying, "We're on the verge of the great tribulation."

- The deceivers and the deceived are saying, "Technology and AI will be the saviour of the world." God is saying, "Jesus Christ is the only Saviour of the world."

I've had many people asking me what about the pandemic? The jab, the big V? Is that all a part of this global deception? Well, when you consider scriptures like *Revelation 18:23* which speaks of the fall of Babylon and the fall of world systems and structures. It reveals that one of the sources of this great end time deception is drugs and pharmaceuticals. Is this an allusion to the big pharmaceutical companies of our times?

Revelation 18:23 says, *The light of a lamp will not shine in you any longer; and the voice of the bridegroom and bride will not be heard in you any longer…because all the nations were deceived by your <u>sorcery</u>. NASB*

The English word "sorcery" here is the Greek word, pharmakeia. The Strong's Concordance defines pharmakeia as; pharmaceutical (the administration of drugs; the use of medicine, drugs or spells)

The Apostle John who under the inspiration of the Holy Spirit leaves us in little doubt that the pharmaceutical industry is, and will be, playing a part in deceiving the nations. The World Health Organisation, an arm of the United Nations, is very much in bed with the pharmaceutical industry. (007) This of course gives the pharmaceutical industry huge influence when it comes to the forming of global policies and international strategies.

So, if the Apostle John is correct, and I believe he is, the pharmaceutical industry is a major player in deceiving the nations.

Another source of this great end time deception is the rapid advances in technology, especially in the area of artificial intelligence. AI will and does have many benefits for humanity, however it also has the means to deceive. AI can make things appear to be real when they're not, or put another way, it can have us believing something is true when it's really a lie. Leading researchers into AI are saying that as this technology advances, the greatest threat it will bring to humanity will be an increasing inability for people to know what is true and what isn't.

While discussing the education of children in schools, an Australian morning TV show (008) revealed that many experts in the AI field are raising concerns that the use of AI in education will have children struggling to know the difference between what's fact and what's fake. AI technology can make things that are not, appear as though they are. It can make things appear to be alive when they're dead. I believe it will be through AI that many of the deceptions Jesus warned about, and the Apostle John wrote about will be realised. John writes in the Book of Revelation that he saw signs and wonders being performed that deceived all those who dwell on the earth. I believe many of these signs and wonders will be worked through AI.

Revelation 13:3 I saw one of his heads as if it had been slain, and his fatal wound was healed. And the whole earth was amazed and followed after the beast. 13 He performs great signs, so that he even makes fire come down out of heaven to the earth in the presence of men. 14 And he deceives those who dwell on the earth because of the signs which it was given him to perform in the presence of the beast 15 And it was given to him to give breath to the image of the beast, so that the image of the beast would even speak… NASB

AI in the hands of those driven by Antichrist motivated globalists will orchestrate these false and deceptive signs and wonders resulting in all of humanity being deceived and following after the beast, the global world power described in the Book of Revelation.

In the movie 'Forrest Gump' which was released in 1994, the character Gump crosses paths with several historical figures, including John F. Kennedy who was assassinated in 1963. The director of the film, Robert Zemeckis used computer-generated effects to insert Forrest into historical scenes, thus making his audience believe that Gump actually did meet with, and speak to, the president. It was an extremely clever deception. How much more so now all these years later can technology with the use of AI create events that look so real, but in reality are a lie. As Jesus said in *Matthew 24:24*, these signs and lying wonders will appear to be so true and real that if possible even the elect could be deceived. There's never been a better time to be alert to the deceit and deceptions the demonic forces are throwing at the world today, including those who are followers of Christ. Here are a few simple steps to help us stand firm and not believe the lies.

<u>Know Your Enemy</u> - Be aware that Satan wants to deceive you. *2 Corinthians 11:14 … Satan himself masquerades as an angel of light.* AMPC

<u>Pray and Stay Humble</u>. *Psalm 25:9 He leads the humble in what is right, and the humble He teaches His way.* AMPC

<u>Read, Study and Learn what the Bible says</u>. *John 17:17 Sanctify them in truth; Thy word is truth.* NASB

<u>Be in fellowship</u> with, and closely connected to mature believers who display the fruit of the Spirit in their lives. *Ecclesiastes 4:12 A person standing alone can be attacked and defeated, but two can stand back-to-back and conquer. Three are even better, for a triple-braided cord is not easily broken.* NLT

Hebrews 10:25 And let us not neglect our meeting together, as some people do, but encourage one another, especially now that the day of His return is drawing near. NLT

It's time to turn to Jesus, repent of your sin, and invite Him to be your Saviour and the Lord of your life.

CHAPTER 6

IT'S ALL SO SCARY

Jesus spoke of worldwide fears when answering His disciple's question about what signs would indicate His coming was near. Jesus said in…

Luke 21:26 "People would be fainting with <u>fear</u> and with <u>foreboding</u> of what is coming on the world… ESV

At the beginning of this book I said I was sitting with my mum and dad watching the Cuban missile crisis unfold and they, along with multiplied millions of people around the world, were afraid this would escalate into WW3.

Since people first walked on the earth they've experienced and encountered things that generate fear. But never has there been a generation like this generation where fear is its constant companion. People all over the world are experiencing distress and troubles caused by fear. Ever since the development of nuclear weapons humanity around the world has never been so fearful. Fearful of…
Global nuclear conflict – Global economic collapse – The

attack on the Twin Towers and the resulting war on terror – Terrorism – North Korean missile testing – China and the USA sabre rattling over the South China Sea – The conflict between Russia and Ukraine, escalating into a war between Russia and NATO allies. The Middle East conflict currently between Israel and Hamas, a war many are saying could draw in other nations and evolve into WW3. On top of all that, there is the international fear of climate change destroying the planet within a few years if a variety of viruses, like SARS, Bird Flu, Swine Flu, Ebola, and the Coronavirus doesn't kill off millions first. The corona virus dominated world media releases for months on end. Travel came to a standstill, countries around the world closed their borders, governments were forcing businesses to close, millions of people lost their employment, and panicked shoppers left grocery store shelves empty. And now we are being warned by the World Health Organisation that we are to expect a more virulent virus in the not too distant future. (009) It'd be true to say that in the midst of all that is happening in the world, there is one underlying disease spreading across the world faster than anything else, and it's called FEAR.

Dr Mark McDonald, a fully certified child, adolescent, and adult psychiatrist, and a medical and legal expert, when being interviewed about the effects of the pandemic on society said, *"We're not in a medical pandemic due to a virus, we're in a <u>pandemic of fear</u>. It's a psychological and emotional pandemic, it took root and multiplied and spread and infected essentially our entire population very rapidly. It still has a very strong foothold here in the United States and* *elsewhere. There are many people, especially in urban areas who are perfectly well physically but they've been paralysed by this grip of fear."* (010)

When speaking of his book, "The United States of Fear – How America Fell Victim to a Mass Delusional Psychosis." Dr McDonald said, *"The original title of my book was 'Pandemic of Fear' and was based exactly on that premise. I've expanded it and changed the title to 'United States of Fear' because I believe that the fear, which you cite accurately as the driving force of this pandemic, has actually expanded far beyond a simple fear. It has moved into terror. It has moved into parallel control. It has moved towards vertical control. And most recently in the United States and other Western democracies, it has moved into purge, meaning anybody who thinks the wrong thing commits wrong think, in the words of George Orwell the author of 1984. And is censored, cancelled, punished, ostracized, removed from society. And I believe ultimately will be imprisoned as the individuals are in some of the other Anglophone countries outside the United States. So children are now simply the latest frontier in my view in the campaign that began with fear and will end with totalitarian control."* (011)

I fully agree with Dr Mark McDonald, that much of what we're seeing taking place in the world today is part of a deliberate strategy and narrative which is intended to generate FEAR in order to get humanity to embrace a New World Order or Global Government. As I stated above, every day the media is bombarding us with news of catastrophic disasters facing our planet that we are going to need saving from. At the time of writing the headlines on the World Economic Forum's Global Cooperation web page was, "The 20 humanitarian crises the world cannot ignore in 2023." (012)

We're being continually reminded of the threat of…
<u>Global</u> Pandemics/Diseases
<u>Global</u> Terrorism, Conflicts and Wars
<u>Global</u> Warming, or now it's called Climate Change
<u>Global</u> Climate Disasters
<u>Global</u> Food Crisis
<u>Global</u> Energy Crisis
<u>Global</u> Economic Crisis

The reality is, this barrage of gloom and doom and impending crises generates fear with a capital F. And if people fear and believe that the planet cannot sustain them. If they believe they will be killed in a nuclear war, or die from a deadly virus. If they believe their kids will grow up in a world of anarchy and terror, and the economy will collapse and they'll lose everything, but the governing authorities say, "It's ok, just do as we say and you'll be safe and secure, we'll protect you." The masses will quickly give up their freedoms and privacy in exchange for security and safety under a global government.

Henry Kissinger, the former National Security Advisor and US Secretary of State understood this. When speaking at a Bilderburg meeting in Evian, France, May 21, 1992, he said, *"The one thing every man fears is the unknown. When presented with this scenario, individual rights will be willingly relinquished for the guarantee of their wellbeing granted to them by their world government."* (013)

Jesus said one of the signs His coming is very near will be men's hearts failing them through fear of what is coming upon the world. That's exactly what we are beginning to see in the world today, so how close is His coming?

It's time to turn to Jesus, repent of your sin, and invite Him to be your Saviour and the Lord of your life.

CHAPTER 7

ONE WORLD – ONE GOVERNMENT

The crises we're seeing around the world are being orchestrated in order to generate enough fear to have people believing the only answer to the problems we're facing is for all nations to come together under a One World Government. We're told it's only in this way will we ever be able to find the answers necessary to live the supposedly utopian way of life the globalists promise. This globalist agenda is driven by the belief that the world is facing many crises and challenges which governments at a national level cannot fully deal with. Because of this the United Nations (UN) Secretary-General, Antonio Guterres, has proposed a plan for countries to surrender sovereignty to the UN in the face of expected future global crises. In a document titled *"Strengthening the International Response to Complex Global Shocks – An Emergency Platform."* (014) Guterres outlines his strategy to enhance global responses to future crises by the means of his *"Emergency Platform."* This platform could be triggered by the Secretary-General at any time during what the UN deems to be a global crisis, requiring nations to become subordinate to the UN and follow all of its demands. In the document Guterres states, *"Recent complex global shocks have shown that, at the global level, our existing, conventional crisis response mechanisms are not up to the task of responding coherently and effectively to global shocks that have an impact on multiple sectors simultaneously. We lack the necessary forums at the global level to tackle multidimensional threats with a multidimensional response. Our existing response architecture, while appropriate for specific events, is too fragmented and sectoral to respond effectively to complex global crises."* The document goes on to say, *"Learning lessons from these recent crises, I propose that the General Assembly provide the Secretary-General and the United Nations system with a standing authority to convene and operationalize automatically an Emergency Platform in the event of a future complex global shock of sufficient scale, severity and reach." (014)*

In other words, what Guterres is saying is we need to have a one world governing body dictating to sovereign nations the course they must take in order to overcome future global crises.

As Bible believing Christians we know that all the troubles facing humanity are due to the fact that mankind has a sin nature and has turned his back on God. Globalists however, would have us believe that man is intrinsically good and can through his own efforts turn the world into a utopian paradise. They believe if they can have all nations come under one government, pooling all of their resources, their knowledge, their technology, their skills and abilities being united and brought together, they can then see all of man's problems being solved and they will literally bring their hoped for socialist utopia to earth. The globalists don't believe in God, they don't think they need God, and they don't want God. They want to be the gods who rule the world.

In March 2023 thought leaders, global experts, government representatives, corporate bosses, and global elites came together in Dubai to plan and put in place strategies for the way the world would be governed into the future. Interestingly enough these movers and shakers named their gathering The World Government Summit. They're not hiding it anymore. The opening welcome address was given by Becky Anderson, a British journalist and one of CNN International's highest profile anchors. She began the summit with these words, *"Ladies and gentlemen, a very very good morning on what is the first official day of the World Government Summit here at Dubai Expo 2023. And the title of this session is, <u>are we ready for a new world order</u>?"* (015)

When the Lord opened a door for the Apostle John to look into the future and see the events that would be unfolding just prior to the Lord's return, he saw what he described as a beast rising to power. He wrote in...

Revelation 13:1-4 I saw a beast coming out of the sea... The dragon (devil) gave the beast his power and his throne and great authority...The whole world was astonished and followed the beast. They worshiped the dragon because he had given authority to the beast, and they also worshiped the beast and asked, "Who is like the beast? Who can make war against him?" 7 He was given authority over every tribe, people, language and nation. 8 All inhabitants of the earth will worship the beast... NASB

So, who is the beast? The Book of Daniel gives us the answer.

Daniel 7:23 Then he said to me, "This fourth beast is the fourth <u>world power</u> that will rule the earth. It will be different from all the others. It will devour the whole world, trampling everything in its path. NLT

Daniel clearly states here the beast isn't a man. The beast of *Revelation 13* isn't the Antichrist it's a WORLD POWER...

This World Power has <u>great power</u>, it has a <u>throne</u>, a place where it exercises its power from, and it has the <u>authority</u> to exercise its power. The beast is a World Government with all power and authority, and it will be led by a man driven by an Antichrist spirit. The Bible calls him, the man of lawlessness, the son of perdition.

If this is the generation that will see the coming of the Lord we should be seeing evidence of this New World Order rising to power, the evidence of a One World Government forming. Well it's becoming increasingly clear that this is exactly what's taking place today. This is one of the reasons why I'm convinced that Jesus is coming back for His church very soon. It's beyond doubt that we are seeing in our lifetime a rapid move toward the establishment of a global totalitarian government. We see nations, especially in the western world, being led by political leaders who all seem to be dancing to a global tune. Rather than making decisions that are best for their own nations and citizens, they appear to be following the directions of the United Nations and its advisory body the World Economic Forum and the World Health Organisation. This influence is evident at every level, national, state and local government.

Consider the policies and decisions national political leaders have been forcing on their people especially over the last few years. Things such as the pandemic lock downs and closures of businesses and schools, mandatory mask wearing, mandatory vaccinations, mandatory social distancing. Now we have the move toward all people receiving a Digital Identity and the push for a Central Bank Digital Currency. The expectation for all of society to accept and celebrate the LGBTQ+ communities and transgenderism. The shutting down and censoring of those speaking out against the globalist agenda and narrative. At the time of writing we are seeing a Misinformation and Disinformation Bill the Australian government is attempting to introduce to silence and censor apposing voices to the globalist agenda. This flows down from the United Nations plans to silence all dissenting narratives. (016) We're seeing the moving away from traditional energy sources due to the threat of so called climate change. Traditional farming and agriculture is being shut down and regulated out of business, the list goes on and on, and all of this is being carried out on a global scale. I think one could be excused for thinking our political leaders are no more than puppets with the strings being pulled by the global elite and global corporations, or as the Apostle John said, "the Beast." This thought of a One World Government or New World Order can no longer be considered a conspiracy theory, though Google will try and tell you it is. Search Google for the New World Order and one of the first thing to come up is... *The New World Order is a conspiracy theory which hypothesizes a secretly emerging totalitarian world government.* (017) But it's hardly a conspiracy theory when we're hearing past and present political leaders, bankers, industrialists and billionaire global elites talking up the need for a New World Order to save the planet. Here are just some of the statements made by world leaders and international influencers over recent years.

- Lawrence Eagleburger, (US Secretary of State to George Bush Snr) stepping down from his role of Secretary of State, writes to his successor saying, *"The world that awaits you is a much different place than the one you and I have known. It is a world in the midst of revolutionary transition, in which you will have an historic opportunity to shape a <u>new international order</u>.* (018)

- Henry Kissinger (former National Security Advisor and Secretary of State) *"The events are so extraordinary around the world his* (Barak Obama) *task will be to develop an overall strategy for America in this period when really a <u>New World Order</u> can be created, it's a great opportunity."* (019)

- Kevin Rudd (Former Australian PM) — *"We see a move of the global geo-economic gravity to Asia. Therefore, I think it's important for us to think through carefully what that means for the <u>global order</u>, the UN, the IMF and other systems." (020)*

- George W Bush Snr (Former US President) —*"What is at stake is more than one small country, it is a big idea, a <u>New World Order</u> where diverse nations are drawn together in a common cause to achieve the universal aspirations of mankind."* (021)

- Winston Churchill *"The creation of an <u>Authoritative World Order</u> is the ultimate aim toward which we must strive."* (022)

- John Howard (Former Australian PM) — March 13, 2003 in an National Address to the nation. *"The decade of the nineteen nineties was meant to have been one in which a <u>New International Order</u>, free of the by polar rivalry of earlier days, was to have been established"* (023)

- Nicolas Sarkozy (Former French President) – *"France intends to pursue together with all people of goodwill around the world this battle to build the <u>New World Order</u> of the 21st century."* (024)

- Bill Clinton (Former US President) —*"After 1989 President Bush said, and it's a phrase I often use myself, is that we need a <u>New World Order</u>."* (025)

- Tony Blair (Former British PM) —*"A new Europe, a <u>New World Order</u>, a new consensus of how life should and could be lived."* (026)

- Gordon Brown (Former British PM) —*"Out of what will be seen as the greatest restructuring of the global economy, perhaps even greater than at the time of the Industrial Revolution, a <u>New World Order</u> will be created."* (027)

- Robert Mueller, sixth director of the Federal Bureau of Investigation. *"We must move as quickly as possible to a <u>one-world government</u>; a <u>one-world religion</u>; under a <u>one world leader</u>."* (028)

- Barack Obama (Former US President) —*"We've gotta win over hearts and minds, we've gotta give them a stake in creating the kind of <u>New World Order</u> that I think all of us would like to see."* (029)

- Joe Biden (US President) – *"Things are shifting, there's going to be a <u>New World Order</u> out there, and we've gotta lead and we gotta unite the rest of the free world in doing it."* (030)

- Brad Hazzard (NSW Minister for Health and Medical Research) *"This is a world pandemic, this is a one in a one-hundred-year event. So, you can expect* *that we will have transmission from time to time and that's just the way it is. We've got to accept that this is a <u>New World Order</u>."* (031)

- Kerry Chant (NSW Chief Health Officer) *"We will be looking at what contact tracing looks like in the <u>New World Order</u>."* (032)

- David Rockefeller (Formally the Director of Council on Foreign relations, Founder of the Trilateral Commission, Member of the Bilderberg Group) *"We are on the verge of Global Transformation, all we need is the right major crisis and the nations will accept a <u>New World Order</u>. Some believe we are part of a secret group of plotters or political conspirators, characterizing my family and me as "internationalists" and of conspiring with others around the world to build a more integrated global political and economic structure –<u>One World</u>, if you will. If that's the charge, I stand guilty and I am proud of it."* (033)

- Pope John Paul II *"By the end of this decade we will live under the first <u>One World Government</u> that has ever existed in the society of nations... a government with absolute authority to decide the basic issues of survival. <u>One world government</u> is inevitable."* (034)

I could go on and on presenting quotes from world leaders speaking of their plans and hopes for a One World Government. But here is just one more quote from…

- John F Kennedy (Former US President) —*"We are opposed around the world by a <u>Monolithic and ruthless conspiracy</u> that relies primarily on covert means* (deception) *for expanding its sphere of influence."* (035)

This was a part of a speech given to a mainstream media group in 1961. I believe JFK's opposition to this monolithic and ruthless conspiracy (NWO) resulted in his assassination in 1963.

It is extremely clear the global elite, the world political leaders and the world media would have us believe we need to embrace this New World Order, or a World Government, in order to save the planet from its problems. But the truth is far from that, the global elite working through the United Nations, the World Economic Forum, and the World Health Organisation have a far more sinister agenda. Their agenda has got nothing to do with saving the planet, it's all about removing the Saviour. Their agenda is to remove God and godliness from the earth. The global elite want to establish themselves as god and have complete control over every human being on earth.

We can see this clearly in Psalm 2. This is a prophetic Psalm where the psalmist David is looking into the distant future and prophesying about events that will take place in the last days. We know this because we read in the Book of Acts where Peter *(Acts 2:17)* is standing before the crowd on the Day of Pentecost declaring that what they are seeing is a "last days" event as spoken of by the prophet Joel. The Bible teaches that the last days began to unfold on the Day of Pentecost when the church was born, and will continue through to when Jesus comes again. Now when we read on to Acts chapter four we see Peter and John being arrested for preaching about Jesus and His resurrection. They are thrown in Jail, beaten and threatened and then released. They immediately go to their companions and pray. Now here's the thing, they start their prayer around David's prophetic Psalm, saying, "David prophesied that this would happen in the last days, that governing authorities would oppose, even with violence, the Christian church" *(Acts 4:25-26)*

Now David's end time prophetic Psalm is far more relevant to us today than at any other time throughout the last 2000 years. He is primarily speaking to those who are living in the last of the last days, those living in the season of Jesus return. As we read David's prophecy below it is clear he is speaking of an Antichrist spirit driven global elite who are conspiring to reject God and His ways.

Psalm 2:1-3 How dare the nations <u>plan</u> a rebellion. Their foolish <u>plots</u> are futile! Look at how the <u>power brokers</u> of the world rise up to hold their <u>summit</u> as the <u>rulers</u>' <u>scheme</u> and <u>confer</u> together against Yahweh and His Anointed King, saying: "Let's come together and break away from the Creator. Once and for all let's cast off these controlling chains of God and His Christ!" TPT

Don't let anybody tell you there isn't a global conspiracy going on. A conspiracy that is certainly not a theory, it's clearly a fact. David is prophesying into the last days and saying there will be power brokers and rulers of the world, planning and plotting and scheming and conferring together.

In other words, they'll be holding their summits and their simulated scenario exercises as they plan and conspire how to do away with what they call the "controlling chains" of God. We who know the Lord would call these controlling chains, "healthy restraints." The boundaries God gives humanity to live by will keep us secure, but these power brokers and rulers of the world are wanting to remove God and all that is godly from the earth and establish their "chains" for humanity. This is why we're seeing in this generation such a turning away from the morals and values God has given us through His word. We're slipping very subtly and incrementally into a world that calls evil what was once considered good, and now calling good what was once considered evil. This turning away from God and His values is not just happening of its own accord, it's being planned and orchestrated by The Beast.

In order to remove all semblance of God and godliness from the earth, these power brokers and rulers would have to remove the Christian church, because the church is the only institution on earth that reminds the world of the existence of God, and the values He gives us to live by. Because of this, the Church is the number one target of the enemy. This would explain why we are seeing governments putting more and more restrictions on churches and religious organisations. And why we're seeing Christians increasingly being ostracised and in many instances, being persecuted in a growing number of countries around the world. The New World Order doesn't want the Christian church around to interrupt its plans for global control. This is all the more reason why it's time for the church to wake up and speak up.

The generation that sees the coming of the Lord should be seeing the formation of an anti-Christian global power, a world government, a New World Order. With the political events unfolding around us, and national governments appearing to be more and more like puppets to the United Nations I think there is very little doubt we're beginning to see the Beast rising in this generation.

It's time to turn to Jesus, repent of your sin, and invite Him to be your Saviour and the Lord of your life.

CHAPTER 8

THE SECOND BEAST

The global elite know they need support to usher in a One World Government. They realise it's going to take a lot more than money to see their plans realised. So where does that support come from, and what is it? Once again, the Bible has the answer. The Apostle John writes...

Revelation 13:11-14 I now saw another beast. This one came out of the ground. It had two horns like a lamb but spoke like a dragon. <u>It worked for the beast</u>...and it used all its authority to force the earth and its people to worship that beast. It worked mighty miracles, and while people watched, it even made fire come down from the sky. This second beast <u>deceived people</u> on earth by working miracles for the first one... CEV/NLT

Note, the word "it" not the word "he" is used seven times here to describe this beast. This second beast isn't a man, just as the first beast isn't a man. So, what is this second beast? Well as we read on we find the answer.

The Second Beast

Revelation 19:20 And the (first) beast was captured, and with him the <u>false prophet</u> who did mighty miracles on behalf of the beast, miracles that <u>deceived</u> all who had accepted the mark of the beast and who worshiped his statue. NLT

There are four things these verses tell us about this second beast.

1—It has a name, its name is the False Prophet
2—It works for the first beast. It causes the whole world to follow and worship the first beast.
3—It is like a lamb. What is a lamb like? A lamb is a gentle creature, it won't bite, it doesn't have fangs, it won't scratch, it doesn't have claws, it wouldn't hurt anyone, it's harmless.
4—It "speaks" like a serpent. The serpent throughout scripture is revealed as Satan. What does Satan speak? Words filled with deception and lies.

The False Prophet will appear to be harmless, but really is a liar and deceiver, a mouthpiece for Satan. He is the exact opposite of a true prophet. A true prophet declares the way things are, and are going to be, truthfully. A false prophet declares the way things are, and are going to be, falsely. And this False Prophet by falsely declaring the way things are, and are going to be, supports and furthers the globalist, One World Government's agenda.

If we are the people living on earth just prior to the return of Jesus Christ we should expect to see the rising up of a global entity, a voice, that has the power to persuade, coerce and deceive the whole world into following an

Antichrist agenda. So, what is the voice being raised in this generation with great global influence that is directing the people of the world to think and act the way they do? I believe it is the <u>WORLD MEDIA</u>. Otherwise known as the Mainstream Media (MSM)

<u>There has never been a time in history where we've had such a powerful global prophetic voice influencing the thoughts, attitudes, actions, and morals of the world like the Mainstream Media does today</u>. Now when I say "Media" I'm not just referring to the major news outlets such as Fox News, MSNBC, BBC, Al Arabiya, Al Jazeera, ABC and CNN, just to name a few. I'm referring to any medium that controls the distribution of news, information and entertainment. For example, Newspapers, magazines, books, movies, video games, music, comics, adult and children TV programs. When you add social media platforms such as Google, X, (Twitter) Facebook, YouTube, Snapchat, Instagram, etc. you have a super powerful voice influencing and directing world opinion and having the power to censor and shut down any other voice that's not supportive of the globalist's agenda. At the time of writing, almost all of what people see, hear and read, through what they believe is an unlimited variety of entertainment and media options, is actually owned by one of six conglomerates. An interesting number don't you think? At the time of writing, these six media giants are known as The Big Six. These Big Six are National Amusement, Disney, Time Warner, Comcast, News Corp, and Sony. Blackrock and Vanguard, the world's largest asset managers, are the two major shareholders.

It's these six conglomerates that control almost all that people hear, see and read. As stated above, there has never been a time in history, there has never been a generation, that has seen such a powerful global voice influencing the thoughts, attitudes, actions, and morals of the world like the world media conglomerates today. This world media conglomeration has been closely supporting the globalist's agenda since the establishment of the United Nations just after WW11.

This media support was made obvious by David Rockefeller when he spoke to the Trilateral Commission in June 1991. He said, *"We are grateful to the Washington Post, The New York Times, Time Magazine, and other great publications (MSM) whose directors have attended our meetings and respected their promises of discretion for almost forty years. It would have been impossible for us to develop our plan for the world if we had been subjected to the lights of publicity during those years. But the world is now more sophisticated and prepared to march towards a one world government."* (036)

What is being said here is this march towards global government is being supported by the world media. At every opportunity, the mainstream media ridicules, attacks, and censors, Christian values, activities and events. Anybody attempting to speak out against the globalist's narrative is censored or silenced. A great example of the power of the media to control the narrative was the silencing of the President of the United States, Donald Trump. President Trump was speaking out against, and exposing the globalist's agenda, resulting in the media shutting him down. Never before in history has a person in such a powerful position been silenced the way he was. Another example of the media shutting down the voices exposing the globalist's evil agenda was the sacking of Tucker Carlson, the most watched conservative political commentator on Fox News. He was a real thorn in the side of the global elite as he showed no fear in shining the light of truth on their lies, so he had to be removed. Satan and his subordinate's plans are built on deception and lies, so anyone challenging those lies must be silenced one way or another.

Paul Joseph Goebbels, minister in charge of Nazi propaganda in WWII said, *"Think of the press as the great keyboard on which the government can play. It's the absolute right of the state to supervise the formation of public opinion...If you tell a lie big enough and often enough people will eventually come to believe it.* (037)

The world media, the False Prophet, is Satan's lying mouthpiece deceiving and influencing humanity to follow his Antichrist agenda. Now some could say, "Oh, but the media releases a lot of material which is true, documentaries, programs, news releases which are absolutely true." That is correct, the MSM does present programming and information that contains truth. But we need to keep in mind that when the devil deceived Eve back in the garden he mixed truth with lies. The Bible tells us the devil is very crafty, he's smart, and he knows what worked with Eve will work today. Mix enough truth with the lies and people will be gullible enough to believe the lie. This is what we're seeing today.

Jesus and the prophets in the Bible have given us signs such as…A nation being born in a day; the fig tree. Israel prospering. A pandemic of deception and lies, creating a pandemic of fear, a fear so great that populations around the world will want to embrace a one world government to keep them safe and secure. An extremely powerful media (the False Prophet) giving full support to the world government's agenda. These signs are becoming increasingly clear, and declare to those who are alert and have eyes to see, that we are in the final countdown to the Second Coming of the Lord Jesus Christ.

It's time to turn to Jesus, repent of your sin, and invite Him to be your Saviour and the Lord of your life.

CHAPTER 9

HYBRID HUMANS

When Jesus was answering His disciple's question regarding the timing of His return He said in...

Matthew 24:36–42 "However, no one knows the day or hour when these things will happen, not even the angels in heaven or the Son himself. Only the Father knows. "When the Son of Man returns, it will be like it was in Noah's day. In those days before the flood, the people were enjoying banquets and parties and weddings right up to the time Noah entered his boat. People didn't realize what was going to happen until the flood came and swept them all away. That is the way it will be when the Son of Man comes. "Two men will be working together in the field; one will be taken, the other left. Two women will be grinding flour at the mill; one will be taken, the other left. "So you, too, must keep watch! For you don't know what day your Lord is coming. NLT

Jesus is obviously speaking here of the rapture of the church. No one knows the day or the hour of this event. Life will be, for many, going on as normal. People will be eating and drinking, they'll be getting married, they'll be living life as normal as one could expect in a rapidly changing world. Then just as Jesus said, suddenly one will be taken and another will be left. The Apostle Paul said this snatching away of the church will happen in the twinkling of an eye. *(1 Corinthians 15:51-52)* This is why we need to be awake and alert to what is taking place in the world, and be ready to meet the Lord because the rapture can take place at any time.

Now when Jesus spoke of this event He said that life on earth at the time of the rapture would be the same as things were back in Noah's day. So, the question we should be asking ourselves is, were there any significant events happening on earth at that time that could be seen as a sign to our generation that the coming of the Lord is near?

The first thing most people would think of when they think of the days of Noah, would be the flood and the ark. I don't believe another flood would be a sign, especially as God promised He would not flood the earth again. The other thing that was obvious in Noah's day was the building of an ark. I'm sure that an ark is not a sign to be looking for either. If people were building an ark to save themselves today they'd be considered to have mental health issues. Another thing the Bible makes very clear is that in Noah's day the world was filled with corruption and wickedness. This is certainly very evident today, although it would be true to say every generation has seen varying degrees of evil. So, were there any other significant events taking place in Noah's day that could speak specifically to our generation? I believe we can find an answer to that in the book of Genesis…

Genesis 6:4 The Nephilim were on the earth in those days, and also afterward, when the sons of God came in to the daughters of men, and they bore children to them. Those were the mighty men who were of old, men of renown. NASB

The International Standard Version calls these mighty men heroes and legendary figures of ancient times.

When I read that, I'm inclined to believe that maybe Greek mythology isn't all myth after all. Perhaps there's more to the legends of Hercules, Achilles, Odysseus and many others than history reveals.

The *Genesis 6:4* scripture is one of the strangest and most challenging scriptures in the Bible. It's clearly saying that in the days of Noah there were half supernatural and half natural human beings. The Bible called them Nephilim, but perhaps another name could be given them, like hybrid humans, or trans-human beings?

The dictionary defines transhumanism as "a philosophy that explores human transcendence above or beyond the organic, through technological and physiological evolution. Not fully human, but having the characteristics of a human being." According to Yuval Noah Harari (more on him shortly) transhumanism revolves around the idea that man has evolved this far, but it's now time for mankind to evolve into a higher level of physical and mental capacity by fusing the physical and mental with AI thus creating superhuman beings.

Now Jesus said that the way life on earth was being lived out in Noah's day, will be seen happening in the generation He's returning to. So as there were hybrid or trans-human beings in Noah's day, and if we are the generation that sees Jesus' return, shouldn't we expect to be seeing hybrid or trans-human beings coming upon the earth? The answer has to be yes.

A person we're hearing a lot about over recent times is Yuval Noah Harari. He is an Israeli intellectual, an author, a historian and Professor in the Department of History at the Hebrew University of Jerusalem. Globalists such as Bill Gates, Barack Obama, Mark Zuckerberg, and many others sing his praises, describing him as 'a prophet in our times.' He has tremendous influence among the movers and shapers of the New World Order, as he is one of the chief advisors to Klaus Schwab, the founder of the World Economic Forum. Because of this he has the ear of multiplied millions of people around the world. He is also an evolutionist. As stated above, he has been called a prophet in our times, but the reality is, he's just one of many false prophets Jesus said would rise up in the last of the last days.

Over the last couple of years, speaking at conferences and through the media he has been recorded saying, *"Humans are now hackable animals. This idea that humans have this soul or spirit and have free will and nobody knows what's happening inside me. So, whatever I choose whether in the election or in the supermarket this is my free will, that's* *over. We are probably one of the last generations of homo-sapiens because in the coming generations we will learn how to engineer body and brain and mind. We have reached the point where we can hack not just computers but human beings as well…By hacking organisms, elites may gain the power to reengineer the future of life itself. Once you can hack something you can usually also engineer it. Science is replacing evolution by natural selection, with evolution by intelligent design. Not an intelligent design by some God above the cloud, but our intelligent design, the intelligent design of our cloud. The IBM cloud, the Microsoft cloud, these are the new driving forces of evolution...We have these two big revolutions, the computer science revolution, and the revolution in biological science, and they are still separate <u>but they are about to merge</u>. Today we have the technology to hack human beings on a massive scale, we are upgrading human beings to gods."* (038)

Regardless of what you might think of the ramblings of Yuval Noah Harari, the reality is mankind is on the verge of creating hybrid human beings, the fusing of the biological with the digital, through advanced technology and artificial intelligence. Governments around the world are actively investigating the technology to create trans-human beings primarily for military purposes. However, it won't stop there, this research into hybrid humans will continue until it touches every sphere of human life. Trans-humanism is I believe another sign telling us Jesus' return is closer than we think.

It's time to turn to Jesus, repent of your sin, and invite Him to be your Saviour and the Lord of your life.

CHAPTER 10

THE MARK OF THE BEAST

The mark of the beast would have to be the most written about, most talked about, most heard of event to take place on earth just prior to Jesus coming again. The mark of the beast is where the global government coerces people to receive a mark or numbering system in order to participate in a digital economy. I don't believe Christians will see this mark being introduced as the church will be taken up in the rapture prior to the mark being forced on humanity. We read about the mark of the beast in…

Rev 13:16-17 And he <u>causes</u> all, the small and the great, and the rich and the poor, and the free men and the slaves, to be given a mark on their right hand or on their forehead, and he provides that no one will be able to <u>buy or to sell</u>, except the one who has the mark… NASB

The receiving of this mark will take place in the days prior to the coming of the Lord Jesus. Therefore, the generation that sees the return of Christ should expect to see technology evolving to a point where it's possible to have all people on earth receive a mark that will govern their ability to buy or sell. I believe the church won't be here to see the mark itself, but the technology making it possible is the sign to be looking for.

There is much debate over what this mark might be, however the scripture above does give some clues into what the mark is, and how it may come about. They tell us all people regardless of their status or social standing will be required to receive the mark. The mark will be forced upon people because if they don't receive it their ability to buy and sell will be taken from them. Also, once received it will permanently align people with a godless Antichrist system. There will be no turning back to God, there is no salvation for those receiving the mark. To understand more about this mark, we also need to consider *Revelation 16:2* which tells us there will be serious health consequences for all who receive the mark.

Revelation 16:2 So the first angel left the Temple and poured out his bowl on the earth, and horrible, malignant sores broke out on everyone who had the mark of the beast... NLT

These scriptures lead me to believe the mark will not be just some form of bar-code stamped on the hand or forehead. But rather something that could be injected into the body, which will eventually result in the breaking out of horrific malignant sores. The Bible tells us the mark will be placed on the right hand or forehead. Why not the upper arm, or neck, or anywhere else on the body? Could the hand and forehead simply be symbolic? After all the Book of Revelation is filled with symbolism. Could the hand be symbolic for our actions, what we do, and the forehead speaks of our mind, our emotions, and the way we think? Could the mark involve nanotechnology being injected into the body bringing about changes to the DNA structure of the body which then would change the way people act and think? If the mark changed the human DNA because it was injected into the body, it would explain why the terrible physical consequences of receiving the mark occur, and also explain why a person who receives it is beyond redemption. If the mark changes the DNA they would no longer be fully human, no longer made in God's image and therefore no longer redeemable.

It is worth noting that the word *on* when speaking of the mark of the beast being *on* the hand and *on* the forehead in *Revelation 13:16* is the Greek word *epi* and can be translated as either *on* or *in*. This explains why translators of the more modern translations of the Bible have chosen to use the word *on* but the translators of older versions of the Bible chose to use the word *in*. For example...

Revelation 13:16 in the King James Bible says, *"And he causeth all, both small and great, rich and poor, free and bond, to receive a mark in their right hand, or in their foreheads." KJV*

Another thought to consider in regarding this, is that most Christians today who are looking for the coming of the Lord are waiting for the temple to be rebuilt in Jerusalem and the Antichrist to enter that temple and display himself as being God, as it is written in *2 Thessalonians 2:4 ...he takes his seat in the temple of God, displaying himself as being God. NASB* But we need to remember that the true temple of God today, isn't a building yet to be built in Jerusalem, it's you. You are the true temple of God today if you are a believer in, and a follower of Jesus Christ. The Apostle Paul makes this so clear in *1 Corinthians 6:19 Do you not know that your body is a temple of the Holy Spirit who is in you… NASB* Note, it's your *body* that's the temple of God, and the Spirit of God dwells *in* your body. Satan wants nothing more than to remove the Spirit of God from the temple and place his Antichrist spirit *in* the temple, in you, in your body. Therefore, I believe it could be nanoparticles injected into the human body that will result in the changing of DNA by fusing the biological and the digital together. This will result in those injected ceasing to bear the image of God, ceasing to be fully human, instead becoming a dwelling for the spirit of Antichrist rather than the Spirit of God. This explains why the "marked" are no longer redeemable. This injection of nanoparticles I believe, is or will carry the mark of the beast, thus allowing or disallowing through digital means the ability to buy and sell. Without this digital mark, you'll be disqualified from engaging in the digital economy.

All of this may sound like a crazy science fiction plot, but please remember Jesus said that if possible the very elect could be deceived by the strategies and schemes of the satanically inspired elite. As I stated above, I believe the mark of the beast will be placed *in*, not *on* humanity, thus connecting them to a satanically driven, digitally connected world. All of this is being introduced subtly and incrementally across the world like a net drawing all of humanity into it. This is why Jesus said over and over again to be on guard, be aware, to stay awake and alert to what's going on around you. The globalist agenda, to enslave humanity by controlling all financial activity through a digital currency and digital tracing system, will I believe, ultimately lead to the mark of the beast.

As it is highly likely that the mark of the beast is something that will be placed *in* a person rather than *on* a person, one must then consider the possibility that the mark will come in the guise of a vaccine being forced upon humanity in order to fight a supposedly new strain of a deadly virus. The penalty for not receiving this vaccine will be the shutting down of your digital bank account thus making it impossible to buy or sell anything. The question is, do we see the technology being developed that could have these things being realised in our generation? I believe the answer is a resounding yes.

The subtle move towards what will ultimately be the mark of the beast will begin with the world government taking steps to remove all cash out of circulation. While we've got cash as a legal tender the elite cannot stop people from buying or selling. So, the start of this plan will be to remove all cash and replace it with a digital economy. The headlines of a main stream media news outlet in Australia recently read "Cashless society unstoppable, expert warns, and it could be here sooner than you think." (039) Over a hundred countries around the world are already moving toward, exploring and piloting a Central Bank Digital Currency. (CBDC). (040) There has never been a generation until now with the technology to go cashless, worldwide.

Along with a digital currency there will be the introduction of a global digital identity system with the capacity to trace every human being on earth. The technology for this could have been in place hundreds of years ago, or years into the far distant future, but it is this generation that has the means to see the mark of the beast rolled out and forced upon humanity around the world.

It's time to turn to Jesus, repent of your sin, and invite Him to be your Saviour and the Lord of your life.

CHAPTER 11

INTERNATIONAL ALLIANCES

One of the clearest prophecies speaking of the events unfolding in the days just prior to Jesus return is the one given by the prophet Ezekiel regarding an alliance of nations coming against Israel. We read that in…

Ezekiel 38:1 And the word of the LORD came to me saying, 2 «Son of man, set your face toward Gog of the land of Magog, the prince of Rosh, Meshech and Tubal, and prophesy against him 3 and say, 'Thus says the Lord GOD, «Behold, I am against you, O Gog, prince of Rosh, Meshech and Tubal. 4 «I will turn you about and put hooks into your jaws, and I will bring you out, and all your army, horses and horsemen, all of them splendidly attired, a great company with buckler and shield, all of them wielding swords; 5 Persia, Ethiopia and Put with them, all of them with shield and helmet; 6 Gomer with all its troops; Beth-togarmah from the <u>remote parts of the north</u> with all its troops—many peoples with you. 7 «Be prepared, and prepare yourself, you and all your companies that are assembled about you, and be a guard for them. 8 «After many days you will be summoned; in the <u>latter years</u>

you will come into the land that is restored from the sword, whose inhabitants have been <u>gathered from many nations</u> to the mountains of Israel which had been a <u>continual waste</u>; but its people were <u>brought out from the nations</u>, and they are living securely, all of them. 9 «You will go up, you will come like a storm; you will be like a cloud covering the land, you and all your troops, and <u>many peoples with you</u>." 10 ‹Thus says the Lord GOD, «It will come about on that day, that thoughts will come into your mind and you will devise an evil plan, 11 and you will say, ‹I will go up against the land of unwalled villages. I will go against those who are at rest, that live securely, all of them living without walls and having no bars or gates, 12 to capture spoil and to seize plunder, to turn your hand against the waste places which are now inhabited, and against the people who are <u>gathered from the nations</u>, who have acquired <u>cattle and goods</u>, who live at the center of the world.' 13 «Sheba and Dedan and the merchants of Tarshish with all its villages will say to you, ‹Have you come to capture spoil? Have you assembled your company to seize plunder, to carry away silver and gold, to take away cattle and goods, to capture great spoil? 14 «Therefore prophesy, son of man, and say to Gog, ‹Thus says the Lord GOD, «On that day when My people Israel are living securely, will you not know it? 15 «You will come from your place out of the <u>remote parts of the north</u>, you and <u>many peoples with you</u>, all of them riding on horses, a great assembly and a mighty army; 16 and you will come up against My people Israel like a cloud to cover the land. It shall come about in the <u>last days</u> that I will bring you against My land… NASB

The Prophet Ezekiel is speaking here about an alliance of nations, most of whom will come from the north of Israel. These nations will come against the land of Israel in the last of the last days, as seen in verse 16 above. It has to be the last of the last days because three times Ezekiel refers to Israel as having been gathered back to the land from many nations. As we saw earlier in chapter 3, Israel was gathered from the nations and returned to their land in 1948. And as there is no historical evidence that this alliance of nations has ever come against Israel prior to that, it's obviously yet to happen at some time in the future.

This alliance of nations is listed as...Magog, Meshech, Tubal, Persia, Ethiopia, Libya, Gomer, Beth-Togarmah. The geographical position of those nations still exists today, however over the centuries some of their names have changed. Most historians believe that <u>Magog</u> is now seen as regions of Russia and Central Asia, including Azerbaijan, Afghanistan, Turkistan, and Kazakhstan. <u>Rosh</u> is now central and northern regions of Russia. <u>Meshech</u> is now Southern Russia, Georgia, and Ukraine. <u>Tubal</u>, <u>Gomer</u> and <u>Beth-Togarmah</u> are now incorporated within the nation of Turkey. <u>Persia</u> has been renamed to become Iran. <u>Ethiopia</u> listed in Ezekiel's prophecy is not the Ethiopia we know today, but is rather Sudan, and <u>Libya</u> is still Libya.

Ezekiel said this military alliance would come against Israel in the last days prior to Jesus return. So, if this is the generation Jesus is returning to we should be seeing evidence of nations, who are opposed to Israel, forming a military alliance.

As biblical prophecy is always 100% accurate, and as the signs we've looked at so far strongly indicate we are the generation Jesus is returning to, it should come as no surprise to see the forming of such a military alliance at this time. In 2001 China and Russia along with Kazakhstan, Tajikistan, Uzbekistan, Kyrgyzstan formed a cultural, economic and military alliance called the Shanghai Cooperation Organisation. (041) The reason for the forming of this international alliance was to give the member nations more open trade opportunities, greater economic stability and to build a military alliance to counter NATO and the USA. Since 2001 India, Pakistan and Iran have become members. Countries who have shown strong interest in becoming members are Afghanistan, Belarus and Mongolia. Other nations with close ties with the Shanghai Cooperative Organisation are Iraq, Syria, Libya and Turkey. So, we are seeing in this generation, not in the distant past, or at some time out there in the far distant future a Communist/Islamic alliance being formed, made up of the nations spoken of by Ezekiel 3000yrs ago. Most of these nations listed in this alliance would love to capture, and carry away the great wealth of Israel as Ezekiel said in his prophecy, and to see Israel fully destroyed. However, as we read on into Chapter 39 of Ezekiel's prophecy, we see that God intervenes and destroys the attacking nations, making this one of the greatest military defeats in history. God will honour His Word which declares Israel will never be driven from its land again.

Ezekiel said in the last days we'll see an alliance of nations coming against Israel, no other generation before us has seen the stage so clearly set for this to happen as this generation.

It's time to turn to Jesus, repent of your sin, and invite Him to be your Saviour and the Lord of your life.

CHAPTER 12

WARS AND
RUMOURS OF WARS

It was the 1st of September 1939 when Germany invaded Poland. Two days later Great Britain and France responded by declaring war on Germany marking the beginning of the war in Europe. The war expanded beyond Europe when just before 8am on Sunday, December 7, 1941 the Japanese attacked Pearl Harbour in Hawaii thus drawing the United States into what became World War 2. The largest and deadliest global conflict in history.

When Jesus was asked by His disciples what will be the sign of your coming and the end of the world. He answered by giving many signs, one of these we see in…

Matthew 24:6-7 "You will be hearing of wars and rumours of wars. See that you are not frightened, for those things must take place, but that is not yet the end. "For nation will rise against nation, and kingdom against kingdom… NASB

The world has seen humans in conflict ever since Cain killed Abel. But, at the time Jesus spoke these words the then known world was in relative peace. It was an enforced peace brought about by the might of the Roman Empire. There were at times tribal and ethnic conflicts throughout the empire, but the military power of Rome would quickly squash any uprisings. However, at the demise of the Roman Empire, starting around AD476, Jesus prophetic words regarding wars and rumours of wars began to be realised. Historical records dating back to the first century, or the beginning of the last days, reveals an ever increasing number of conflicts and wars. But, it is in this generation we have seen the greatest number of conflicts and wars than at any other time in history. It has also been the bloodiest generation in history. We have seen more people being killed in this generation through war than any other time in human history. Below is a list (not complete) of conflicts and wars from World War 2 to the present day, with the estimated number of people killed.

- 1939–1945 - <u>World War II</u> 60,669,200 - 84,589,300

- 1947–1948 - <u>Indo-Pakistani War</u> 2,604 - 7,000

- 1948 - <u>Costa Rican Civil War</u> 2,000

- 1945–1949 - <u>Indonesian National Revolution</u> 200,000–400,000

- 1945–1949 - <u>Greek Civil War</u> 45,000

- 1947–1949 - <u>1948 Palestine War</u> 14,400–24,400

- 1950–1953 - <u>Korean War</u> 1,200,000—3,000,000

- 1946-1954 - <u>First Indochina War</u> 1,000,000

- 1956 - <u>Suez War</u> 3,203

- 1948-1960 - <u>La Violencia</u> 180,000–300,000

- 1948-1960 - <u>Malayan Emergency</u> 11,053

- 1952-1960 - <u>Mau Mau Uprising</u> 14,077

- 1960-1961 - <u>Boudica</u>'s uprising 70,000

- 1954-1962 - <u>Algerian War of Independence</u> 100,000–1,000,000

- 1962 - <u>Sino-Indian War</u> 4,600

- 1960-1965 - <u>Congo Crisis</u> 100,000—200,000

- 1965 - <u>Indo-Pakistani War</u> 7,264–10,000

- 1965 - <u>Dominican Civil War</u> 3,533

- 1967 - <u>Six-Day War</u> 14,000–24,483

- 1969 - <u>Sino-Soviet border conflict</u> 159+

- 1967-1970 - <u>Nigerian Civil War</u> 1,000,000-3,000,000

- 1962-1970 - <u>North Yemen Civil War</u> 150,000

- 1967-1970 - <u>War of Attrition</u> 5,573–13,521

- 1971 - <u>Bangladesh Liberation War</u> 300,000–3,000,000

- 1971 - <u>Indo-Pakistani War</u> 23,384

- 1955-1972 - <u>First Sudanese Civil War</u> 500,000

- 1972 - <u>Frist Burundian Civil War</u> 300,000

- 1973 - <u>Yom Kippur War</u> 10,000–21,000

- 1974 - <u>Turkish invasion of Cyprus</u> 5,000

- 1953-1975 - <u>Laotian Civil War</u> 70,000+

- 1967-1975 - <u>Cambodian Civil War</u> 200,000—300,000

- 1975-1978 - <u>Indonesian invasion of East Timor</u> 100,000–200,000

- 1977-1978 - <u>Ethio-Somali War</u> 6,500+

- 1964-1979 - <u>Rhodesian Bush War</u> 30,000

- 1978-1979 - <u>Iranian Revolution</u> 2,781

- 1978-1979 - <u>Uganda–Tanzania war</u> 2,000

- 1979 - <u>Sino-Vietnamese War</u> 30,000

- 1979-1982 - <u>Islamic uprising in Syria</u> 26,500-87,000

- 1982 - <u>First Lebanon War</u> part of the <u>Lebanese Civil War</u> 28,000

- 1982 - <u>Falklands War</u> 874

- 1976-1983 - <u>Dirty War</u> 9,000+

- 1983-1984 - <u>Mountain War (Lebanon)</u> 1,600

- 1979-198 - <u>Ugandan Bush War</u> 500,000

- 1986-87 - <u>Toyota War</u> part of the <u>Chadian-Libyan conflict</u> 8,500

- 1980-1988 - <u>Iran–Iraq War</u>/<u>First Persian Gulf War</u> 1,000,000

- 1987-1988 - <u>Thai-Laotian Border War</u> 1,000+

- 1992 - <u>War of Transnistria</u> 1,643—2,237

- 1996-1997 - <u>First Congo War</u> 800,000

- 1977-1989 - <u>Cambodian–Vietnamese War</u> 175,300

- 1979-1989 - <u>Soviet war in Afghanistan</u> 957,865—1,622,865

- 1989 - <u>Romanian Revolution</u> 1,500

- 1975-1990 - <u>Lebanese Civil War</u> 150,000–170,000

- 1961-1991 - <u>Eritrean War of Independence</u> 570,000

- 1972-91 - <u>Nicaraguan Revolution</u> 60,000

- 1974-1991 - <u>Ethiopian Civil War</u> 230,000–1,400,000

- 1990-1991 - <u>Second Persian Gulf War/Operation Desert Storm</u> 40,000–57,000

- 1991 - <u>Uprisings in Iraq</u> 85,000-235,000

- 1979-1992 - <u>Salvadoran Civil War</u> 78,000-88,000

- 1991-1992 - <u>South Ossetia War</u> 1,000

- 1990-1993 - <u>Rwandan Civil War</u> 800,000–1,000,000

- 1992-1993 - <u>War in Abkhazia</u> 20,000+

- 1964-1974 - <u>Mozambican War of Independence</u> 63,500—88,500

- 1975-1994 - <u>Mozambican Civil War</u> 900,000–1,000,000

- 1988-1994 - <u>Nagorno-Karabakh War</u> 30,000+

- 1994 - <u>Zapatista uprising</u> in Chiapas 1,000

- 1994 - <u>1994 civil war in Yemen</u> 7,000–10,000

- 1991-1995 - <u>Croatian War of Independence</u> 15,000–20,000

- 1991-1995 - <u>Yugoslav Wars</u> 116,000-500,000

- 1992-1995 - <u>Bosnian War</u> 104,000—250,000

- 1992-1997– <u>Tajikistan Civil War</u> 50,000–100,000

- 1960-1996 - <u>Guatemalan Civil War</u> 200,000

- 1989-1996 - <u>First Liberian Civil War</u> 220,000

- 1994-1996 - <u>First Chechen War</u> 50,000–200,000

- 1997 - <u>Albanian Rebellion</u> 3,800

- 1990-1998 - <u>Bougainville Conflict</u> 15,000—20,000

- 1997-1999 - <u>Republic of the Congo Civil War</u> 13,929

- 1998-1999 - <u>Guinea-Bissau Civil War</u> 655+

- 1998-1999 - <u>Kosovo War</u> 2,000–7,000

- 1999 - <u>Kargil War</u> 1,227—5,600

- 1998-2000 - <u>Eritrean-Ethiopian War</u> 125,000

- 1999-2000 - <u>East Timorese crisis</u> 1,400

- 1989-2001 - <u>Civil war in Afghanistan</u> 400,000

- 1992-2001 - <u>Sierra Leone Civil War</u> 200,000

- 1975-2002 - <u>Angolan Civil War</u> 500,000

- 1991-2002 - <u>Algerian Civil War</u> 200,000

- 1918-2003 - <u>Iraqi–Kurdish conflict</u> 138,800—320,100

- 1998-2003 - <u>Second Congo War</u>/Great War of Africa 2,500,000—5,400,000

- 1999-2003 - <u>Second Liberian Civil War</u> 150,000—300,000

- 1983–2005 - <u>Second Sudanese Civil War</u> 1,000,000

- 1993-2005 - <u>Second Burundian Civil War</u> 300,000

- 2006 - <u>Second Lebanon War</u> 1,500

- 1975-2007 - <u>Insurgency in Laos</u> 100,000

- 1999-2007 - <u>Ituri conflict</u> 60,000

- 2002-2007 - <u>Civil war in Côte d'Ivoire</u> 3,000

- 1995-2008 - <u>Insurgency in Ogaden</u> 8,500

- 2008 - <u>Russia–Georgia war</u> 1659—2,496

- 1983-2009 - <u>Sri Lanka/Tamil conflict</u> 60,000

- 1999-2009 - <u>Second Chechen War</u> 54,402—74,402

- 2008-2009 - <u>Gaza War</u> 1,179—1,430

- 2005-2010 - <u>Chadian Civil War</u> 1,310—2,026

- 2010 - <u>South Kyrgyzstan ethnic clashes</u> 2,000

- 1959-2011 - <u>Basque conflict</u> 1,229

- 2010-2011 - <u>Second Ivorian Civil War</u> 3,000

- 2011 - <u>Libyan civil war</u> 25,000–30,000

- 2011-2012 - <u>Yemeni Revolution</u> 2,000

- 1979-2013 - <u>Kurdish–Turkish conflict</u> 45,000

- 2012-2013 - <u>Northern Mali conflict</u> 3,524

- 2013 - <u>Political violence in Egypt</u> 1,119

- 2001-2021 - <u>War in Afghanistan</u> 47,246—61,603

- 1918–present - <u>Iranian-Kurdish conflict</u> 34,000

- 1920–present - <u>Arab-Israeli conflict</u> 115,311

- 1942–present - <u>Communist insurgency in the Philippines</u> 43,388

- 1948–present - <u>Internal conflict in Burma</u> 210,000

- 1948–present - <u>Balochistan conflict</u> 16,765 - 17,065

- 1953–present - <u>Nigerian Sharia conflict</u> 15,000

- 1954–present - <u>Ethnic conflict in Nagaland</u> 34,000

- 1964–present - <u>Colombian conflict</u> 600,000

- 1964–present - <u>Insurgency in Northeast India</u> 25,000

- 1967–present - <u>Naxalite-Maoist insurgency</u> 13,812

- 1969–present - <u>Islamic insurgency in the Philippines</u> 120,000

- 1970–present - <u>Western Sahara conflict</u> 14,000—21,000

- 1980–present - <u>Internal conflict in Peru</u> 69,000

- 1987–present - <u>Lord's Resistance Army insurgency</u> 200,000—500,000

- 1988–present - <u>Somali Civil War</u> 550,000

- 1989–present - <u>Kashmiri insurgency</u> 41,000—100,000

- 1989–present - <u>Xinjiang conflict</u> 2,000—3,000

- 1992–present - <u>Al-Qaeda insurgency in Yemen</u> 3,699

- 1994–present - <u>Cabinda conflict</u> 1,000—1,500

- 2001–present - <u>War on Terror</u> 272,000—329,745

- 2002–present - <u>Insurgency in the Maghreb</u> 6,000

- 2003–present - <u>War in Darfur</u> 178,258—461,520

- 2004–present - <u>War in North-West Pakistan</u> 45,852—78,946

- 2004–present - <u>South Thailand insurgency</u> 5,469

- 2004–present - <u>Conflict in the Niger Delta</u> 4,000—10,000

- 2004–present - <u>Shia insurgency in Yemen</u> 25,000

- 2006–present - <u>Mexican Drug War</u> 106,800+

- 2009–present - <u>Sudanese nomadic conflicts</u> 5,641

- 2009–present - <u>South Yemen insurgency</u> 1,554

- 2009–present - <u>Insurgency in the North Caucasus</u> 2,198

- 2011–present - <u>Syrian civil war</u> 100,000—120,000

- 2011–present - <u>2011–present Libyan factional fighting</u> 1,371—1,397

- 20011- present - <u>Sudan internal conflict (2011–present)</u> 2,557

- 2011 - present - <u>Iraqi insurgency (post-U.S. withdrawal)</u> 8,136+ (042)

- 2022 to present – Russia invades Ukraine – 190,000+ (043)

- 2023 present – Hammas invades Israel – 9,000+

This horrific number of wars and conflicts, and the number of people killed is a terrible reminder of the state of humanity because of its rejection of God.

As we move closer to the last of the last days, we are seeing an ever increasing number of hostilities and conflicts. At the time of writing another war has just erupted in the Middle East. The Palestinian terrorist group known as Hamas attacked Israel, with Israel responding with air and land forces attacking and taking ground in the Gaza Strip. The fear is that other nations will become involved causing an escalation in the fighting. When we look at the dates and times of the conflicts listed above, I believe it would be true to say there has not been a time where wars and conflicts have not ceased since Israel returned to Palestine in 1948.

Jesus said a sign of His soon return would be wars and 'rumours' of wars. The Greek word for 'rumours' here is *akoē* which means to *hear* or *talk of* or *news* of war. This is so true of today. There would not be a day go by where the media is not reminding us of conflicts now happening or likely to happen. Virtually every day we are hearing of China's threat to take Taiwan by military force. The sabre rattling between China and America over Taiwan and the South China Sea. The war in Ukraine escalating into World War 3. Israel threatening to take out nuclear sites in Iran. Possible conflict between Iran and Saudi Arabia. Possible conflict over disputed territories in India's north with Pakistan and China. North Korea threatening war with the United States. The list goes on and on.

Was Jesus speaking of this generation more than any other when He said, "There'll be wars and rumours of wars?" I believe He was. The nonstop conflicts and growing hostilities we are seeing between nations is I believe another sign the Lord gave to reveal that His coming is near.

CHAPTER 13

WE'RE ALL ON THE MOVE

At the age of twelve I learnt to drive a car. My parents had an old Vanguard and my dad would let me drive it around the streets of our town. I had to sit on a cushion to see out the windscreen and have the seat as far forward as possible to reach the pedals. The fact that I managed to not hit a single vehicle I was sharing the road with wasn't necessarily my limited driving skills, but more to the fact that there were so few cars on the road back then. Wow how times have changed. Skilful and alert driving is essential to avoid collisions on today's roads because the volume of traffic has grown exponentially. As of January 2021, there were 20.1 million registered vehicles on Australian roads. (044) Is it little wonder we're constantly reminded to stay alert and slow down.

It's not just by motor vehicles that millions of people all over the world are travelling. In India alone 23 million people travel on trains every day. (045) Yes, that's right, every day.

People are constantly on the move. My wife and I have been privileged to travel to many parts of the globe. Virtually every airport we fly into or depart from regardless of where it is in the world, is filled with people just like us, arriving and departing. Humanity around the world is on the move in this generation more than ever before.

The number of commercial flights travelling in the skies across the earth in 2019 was 38.9 million. This vast amount of travel was halted for a season due to the covid pandemic which grounded airlines around the world. Before the pandemic it was expected that in 2020 a new record of 4.5 billion passengers would be flying in 40.3 million commercial flights. (046) That is over half of the world's population. Since the covid restrictions are now being lifted, we are once again seeing a continuing escalation in air travel. Is it any wonder you have to stand in line at airports? It's not just air travel that's seeing massive numbers or people travelling. The cruise ship industry is seeing rapid growth in the number of holiday makers taking to the seas. In 2019, 29.7 million people spent their holidays on the open seas. (047)

It's in this generation that people have been on the move more than at any other time in history. Could it be that the record number of people travelling, by whatever the means, are more than just interesting statistics. We read in the book of Daniel…

Daniel 12:4 "But you, Daniel, keep these words secret, and seal the book until the end times. Many will <u>*travel*</u> <u>*everywhere*</u>*, and knowledge will grow." GW*

The Bible makes a clear link here between a generation that will see a rapid increase in travel and the end times. Is the exponential growth in travel we're seeing today, another sign that we're the generation living at the end of the age and therefore will witness the coming of the Lord? I believe it is.

It's time to turn to Jesus, repent of your sin, and invite Him to be your Saviour and the Lord of your life.

CHAPTER 14

WE KNOW SO MUCH MORE

In writing this book I'm sitting here at my computer typing out my thoughts. I'm not writing my thoughts with a fountain pen or its predecessor a dip pen, or the predecessor to that, the quill pen. How things have changed, technology is advancing, and with the advancements in artificial intelligence knowledge is increasing at an exponential rate. When I was a kid I had to walk to a red phone box with my small coins to make a call, usually with the help of an operator who would put the call through for me. Now I just have to tap my iPhone to speak to people anywhere in the world.

It's been in my lifetime that we've moved on from phone boxes to iPhones, from the monocular to the Hubble Telescope, from steam trains to 300km/hr electric trains, from Encyclopaedia Britannica to Google and Wikipedia and now we are moving into the world of artificial intelligence. I've seen us go from paper road maps to on board satellite navigation, from steam power to nuclear power, from the Biplane to the Airbus A380 and now space travel. We have seen, in this generation, exponential growth in knowledge in the fields of technology, medicine and science.

This is what's written in the book of Daniel about this increased growth in knowledge...

Daniel 12:4 But you, Daniel, keep these words secret, and seal the book until the <u>end times</u>. Many will travel everywhere, and <u>knowledge will grow</u>." GW

Or as the New Living Translation puts it... ...<u>*knowledge will increase*</u>.

The word *"increase"* does not mean an addition of knowledge, but an <u>exponential</u> growth in knowledge.

In 1982 Buckminster Fuller created the "Knowledge Doubling Curve"; (048) he noticed that until 1900 human knowledge doubled approximately every century. By the end of World War II knowledge was doubling every 25 years. If you think you are overwhelmed with information right now, I can assure you there's more to come. IBM had predicted that by 2020, knowledge will likely be doubling every 11 to 12 *hours*.

The prophet Daniel made it clear that this exponential growth in knowledge would be seen by the generation living at the end of time.

It's time to turn to Jesus, repent of sin, and invite Him to be your and Saviour and the Lord of your life.

Jesus gave sign after sign, to those who are awake and looking for them, to reveal just how close His coming is. He spoke of Israel returning to their homeland and experiencing great prosperity just prior to His return. A pandemic of fear spreading across the earth. A global government forming, being supported by a false prophet. He spoke of the days of Noah and hybrid humans. A mark that will finally determine where people's allegiances truly are. An international military alliance coming against Israel. Exponential growth in travel and knowledge. Jesus said (*Matthew 24:33-34*) the generation that sees these signs or events unfolding, or the stage being set for them to unfold, will know that His coming is very near, He is at the very door. We are seeing in this generation these signs materialising before our very eyes. How close to the end are we? As we look further into God's Word we see even more evidence that points to the imminent return of our Lord and Saviour Jesus Christ.

CHAPTER 15

PERSECUTION OF BELIEVERS

Persecution of the followers of Christ has been seen in every generation since Jesus walked the earth 2000 years ago. We shouldn't be surprised by that as Jesus himself said in...

John 15:19-20 "If you were of the world, the world would love its own; but because you are not of the world, but I chose you out of the world, because of this the world hates you. "Remember the word that I said to you, 'A slave is not greater than his master.' If they persecuted Me, they will also persecute you... NLT

From the middle of the 20th century through to the present day the heaviest persecution of Christians has been seen most in countries like North Korea, China, India, Pakistan, North Africa, and the Middle East. But it's only been in more recent times, in this generation, we are seeing a growing number of reports of persecution, hostility and ill-treatment coming out of, not just the communist and Islamic nations but from nations who were once supportive or at least tolerant of Christianity. We are regularly seeing reports through the media of people being arrested, and jailed, for speaking out and living out their faith.

There's the case of Pavia Räsänen, a devout Christian and member of the Finnish Parliament, faces a criminal trial for openly stating her faith. (049) Then you have Canadian Pastor Artur Pawlowski arrested and jailed for holding church services during the covid pandemic. (050) Canadian Pastor Derek Reimer is arrested for speaking out against a drag queen story time event for kids at a public library. (051) Pastor John Sherwood was arrested in west London, England for preaching what police say was an 'offensive' message from the Bible. (052) American football coach Joe Kennedy, was fired from his job after conducting prayer sessions with his team. (053) A 2017 survey conducted by Public Religion Research Institute found that millions of Americans, including 57% of white evangelical Protestants, say that "there is a lot of discrimination" against Christians in the U.S. today. (054) In Australia there is growing resistance to Christian ethics and practises. An example of this was the Australian Capital Territory Government's take over of the Catholic Calvary Hospital because it refused to perform abortions. (055) There's increasing tensions in Australia between Christian schools and government requirements regarding sexuality and non-discrimination. Christian schools are being increasingly pressed to conform to radical sexual and gender ideology. (056) Australian politician Bob Katter claimed Christianity is under attack in Australia when he cited how seven Christian professional football players were stood down by their club because they refused to wear the LGBTQ+ pride uniforms on 'religious grounds'. (057) These are just a few examples of the growing hostilities towards Christians in the once "religiously safe" western world.

We are seeing in this generation that persecution and hostility toward Christians is no longer limited to just Islamic and Communist countries but is now being experienced by believers around the world. This is another sign of the drawing near of the Lord's coming. Jesus spoke of this in...

Matthew 24:8-9 "But all this is only the first of the birth pains, with more to come. Then you will be arrested, persecuted, and killed. You will be <u>hated all over the world</u> because you are my followers." NLT

We are now beginning to see these prophetic words of Jesus coming to pass. Never before have we seen a worldwide turning away from Christian values, and a turning against those who hold to those values. As stated above the nations which were once considered bastions of Christianity such as America, the United Kingdom, New Zealand, Australia, and across Europe, are now turning away from the very foundations that made their countries great. The Christian church is, like never before, being targeted not just by the media and radical left-wing groups, but also the governments of these western countries. Many political leaders and authorities are beginning to align various Christians and Christian organisations with extremist groups and in some instances even labelling them terrorists. (058)

Historically we've always seen hostilities and persecution against Christians all over the world, but it's in this generation we are seeing that ramping up dramatically. Open Doors International, a Christian ministry supporting persecuted Christians around the world says, "360 million people suffer high levels of persecution and discrimination for their faith in the world today, and that number is growing rapidly." (059) Christians are now facing severe persecution in 61 countries. (060) The Pew Research Centre has reported that the number of countries where Christians are subject to a degree of government-enforced restrictions and communal hostility has grown from 108 in 2014 to 143 in 2017. (061)

Jesus said, *(Matthew 24:8-9)* The generation that sees the rapid increase of persecution against believers around the world should see this as another sign that His return is very close.

It's time to turn to Jesus, repent of sin, and invite Him to be your Saviour and the Lord of your life.

CHAPTER 16

GOOD NEWS FOR ALL NATIONS

One of the reasons for the increase in persecution is because the church is growing around the world. (We'll look at this more closely in the next chapter) Because of this growth, the Gospel is also spreading rapidly to all nations. This again is another sign that the Lord's return is drawing very near. Jesus said in…

Matthew 24:14 "And this gospel of the kingdom will be proclaimed throughout the whole world as a testimony to all nations, and then the end will come." NASB

This is clearly another sign Jesus gave that is being realised in this Generation. What Jesus is saying is the generation that sees the Gospel being taken to all people groups and races of the world, that generation will see the coming of the Lord.

Never before in history has there been such a push by missionary organisations and churches to see the Gospel reaching every nation on earth. The word "nation" here is the Greek word "ethnos" which is where we get the word "ethnic" from, meaning people groups or races.

One thing we need to be aware of here is that the Gospel will eventually reach every people group on earth, but that doesn't necessarily have to happen before the rapture takes place. You see when Jesus spoke of the end coming, He was speaking about His literal bodily return to the Mount of Olives and the final defeat of Satan and all who follow him, and therefore, the end of the world as we know it. However, the Lord will come for His Bride (Church) and meet her in the air, well before the final end, this is called the rapture, or the snatching away, or the taking up of the church. (*1 Thessalonians 4:16-18, 1 Cor 15:51-52*) After the church has gone the Gospel will continue to be preached. The Book of Revelation in Chapter 7 speaks of 144,000 who are sealed for service. In the same chapter, and perhaps because of the 144,000, we read of the multitudes of people of all races, tribes and languages coming out of the Great Tribulation and worshiping God in heaven. We also read in *Revelation 11:3-9* about the Two Witnesses prophesying and sharing their testimony for 1260 days, this again could speak of the Gospel being proclaimed around the world, especially as the scripture indicates that all on the earth shall both hear them and see them.

Even though it appears the preaching of the Gospel will continue well after the church has ascended to heaven. I must hasten to add that we should never hold back from sharing our faith with others and taking the Gospel to the world. And the exciting thing is, that is happening at an exponential pace. Never before in history has the church had the means to take the Gospel to every people group like it has in this generation. With the aid of technology such as satellite communication the Gospel is now being taken into parts of the world that have never been accessible before. Christian satellite TV channels are virtually reaching in to almost every nation on earth, and therefore making huge inroads into previously unreached people groups. For the first time in history the church has the means to take the Gospel to every people group on earth. This is another clear sign that we are the generation to see the coming of the Lord.

It's time to turn to Jesus, repent of your sin, and invite Him to be your Saviour and the Lord of your life.

CHAPTER 17

THE RISING OF
THE CHURCH

When Jesus returns in the air to take His bride home, He'll be returning to a church that is rising in influence and radiance as the world spirals downward into ever increasing spiritual darkness and decay.

Isaiah prophecies of the last days saying in...*Isaiah 60:1-3 Arise, shine; for your light has come, and the glory of the LORD has risen upon you. For behold, darkness will cover the earth and deep darkness the peoples; But the LORD will rise upon you and His glory will appear upon you... NASB*

Now some believe that Jesus return will usher in a thousand years of peace, blessing and prosperity, where Jesus will rule and reign upon the earth, they call this The Millennium. I'll leave it to others to investigate that topic. But there are those who believe the Isaiah Chapter 60 scriptures above are speaking of that thousand years, I don't believe that is the case, simply because Isaiah speaks of darkness covering the earth and deep darkness the people. The two words "darkness" here aren't speaking of a physical night time darkness, the words literally mean "gross wickedness, evil, misery and despair" which Isaiah said, "Will cover the earth." The Millennium will be a time of light, liberty and freedom, no darkness at all. Therefore, I believe the Isaiah Chapter 60 prophecy above is speaking of the time just prior to the second coming of Jesus Christ.

As we saw earlier, Jesus said in...*Matthew 24:37, When the Son of Man comes again, it will be exactly like the days of Noah.* GW

In Noah's day, the world was dark and growing darker, and more was happening than hybrid humans being born to women. In the midst of the darkness, the ark was being built. I believe the Old Testament story of Noah building his ark is a perfect picture seen in the New Testament of Jesus building His Church. The ark was God's grace revealed, the church is God's grace revealed. The ark was conceived, orchestrated and inspired by the Holy Spirit, but it took human involvement to build it. The church is conceived, orchestrated and inspired by the Holy Spirit, but it takes human involvement to build it. God instructed Noah and all his family to build the ark, God instructs all His family to build the church. The ark was built according to God's plan, the church is being built according to God's plan. God miraculously called animals of all shapes, sizes, species and colours into the ark. God is miraculously calling people of all shapes, sizes, colours and races into the church. The ark was built to withstand the wildest storms, the church is being built to withstand the wildest storms, in fact it can stand against all the enemy throws at her. (*Matthew 16:18*) Noah and his family and the animals were destined to die in the flood if they didn't enter the ark, but they lived and were kept safe because they did enter. The people who come into the church were destined to die, but by becoming a part of the church they live and find newness of life. The ark had everything necessary to sustain life, the church has everything necessary to sustain this new life. The ark's timbers were covered over with tar or pitch. (*Genesis 6:14*) The Hebrew word for pitch is Kophar which figuratively means a redemptive price, to ransom, to cover over. The pitch was to cover over or redeem the imperfections of the timber being built into the ark. The church is covered over with a redemptive price. When a person is built into the church the blood of Jesus covers us, it cancels out, it pardons, the imperfections in our lives. The ark had only one way in, through the one door. The church has only one way in, through the one door and Jesus said, He is that door. The ark had many rooms, Jesus said, "In my Father's House (the Church) there are many rooms." The ark rose above the darkness, devastation, misery and despair flooding the earth. It was the only place where life was saved. The ark is a picture of the end time church and Jesus said, as it was in Noah's day so shall it be at the time of His return.

Today we're seeing the spiritual ark, the church, rising above the darkness, devastation, misery and despair flooding the world. The church is rising in influence and prominence and will become the most influential and prominent institution on earth.

Micah 4:1 In the last days, the Temple of the Lord (The Church) *will become the most important place on earth.* NLT

Ephesians 1:23 The church, is not peripheral to the world; the world is peripheral to the church. MSG

Now this might seem contradictory to what you have just read in chapter fourteen regarding the church being heavily persecuted. Yes, persecution will increase against the church, but persecution won't decimate the church, it will consolidate and strengthen it. Historically persecution against the church has almost always brought about numerical growth, and has made it stronger and more determined to advance. When I look at what the church has become and is becoming, it's nothing more than miraculous. I believe we are seeing the *Isaiah 60:1-2* prophecy being fulfilled in this generation.

When I was a child, the Church was considered to be insignificant, irrelevant, and shrinking, but now its rising and shining and getting brighter every day. The media would have us believe that the Christian church is in decline, don't believe the lie, the church is growing exponentially around the world.

This amazing last days growth of the church has come about just as Jesus said it would. *Matthew 13:39 ...The harvest is the close and consummation of the age... AMPC*

Jesus is speaking here of a great end time harvest, He's speaking of a turning to God's Kingdom by people all over the world, and this turning, this flood of humanity coming to Christ will be a clear sign that we are at the threshold of Jesus return and the end of the age. Therefore, the generation that sees Jesus return should expect to see a harvest of souls coming in, in that generation. Are we seeing that in this generation? I believe we are. Here are some of the amazing things God has done, and is doing in the building of His church around the world. You'll never read or hear any of this from the mainstream media.

Wes Granberg-Michaelson, who served for 17 years as general secretary of the Reformed Church in America, states that over the past 100 years, Christianity grew from less than 10 percent of Africa's population to over 500 million today. (062)

Asia is also experiencing growth. In the last century, Christianity grew at twice the rate of the population in that continent. Asia's Christian population of 350 million is projected to grow to 460 million over the next 6 years. (063)

Christianity Today reports that the Church has seen dramatic and explosive growth in Asia, Africa and South America. The growth of the African Church in particular is jaw-dropping. In 1900 there were fewer than 9 million Christians in Africa. Now there are more than 541 million. In the last 15 years alone, the Church in Africa has seen a 51 percent increase, which works out on average at around 33,000 people either becoming Christians or being born into Christian families each day in Africa alone. Over the last 40 years evangelists Reinhard Bonnke and Daniel Kolenda along with the Christ for all Nations ministries in Africa have seen 88 million salvation decision cards handed in by people giving their lives to Christ in their crusades. (064)

World Magazine writer Warren Cole Smith interviewed 25 year missionary David Garrison who has documented his findings about the massive number of Muslims converting to Christianity. "There is a revival in the Muslim world," Garrison says, "Up to 7 million former Muslims have converted to Christianity in the past two decades." (065)

It was estimated that the number of Christian converts from a Muslim background in Iran was between 5,000 and 10,000 people, today that's between 800,000 to 1 million people.

According to International Missions News, Iran has the fastest growing evangelical movement in the world. (066)

Never before throughout all the generations that have gone before us has there ever been such a turning to Christ by so many people groups.

At the beginning of the twentieth century it was estimated that the number of Christians living in South Korea was only 0.1% of the population. Today it is believed that almost one third of the population is Christian. (067)

Brazil has seen a massive growth in Protestant Christianity. In just ten years from 2000 to 2010 Christianity grew from 26 million (15%) in 2000 to 42 million (22%) in 2010. Today it is estimated that the Christian population is 70 million or nearly one third of the Brazilian population. (068) (069)

Most people have heard of the growth of Christianity in China, but many don't understand how exponential that growth has been. Over the last thirty years the number of Christians has grown from just under ten million to almost one hundred and ten million by 2020, and the growth rate is continuing. (070)

India has become the most populous nation on earth, surpassing China's population of 1.4 billion. The predominant religion in India is Hindu, followed by Islam, but Christianity is seeing rapid growth. In 2012 it was estimated that 2.5% of the population was Christian, but that number is now estimated at about 5.8% today. (071)

In 1951 there were no Christians in Nepal and just 458 people professed to be Christian by 1961. But by 2011, there were nearly 376,000, and the latest census estimates the Christian population is now around 545,000. (072)

The Centre for the Study of Global Christianity at Gordon-Conwell Theological Seminary in their Status of Global Christianity 2022 report states, "Globally Christianity is growing faster than the population growth rate. In 2022, Christianity was growing at a 1.27% rate, taking the total number of Christians in the world to an estimated 2.56 billion, almost a third of the world's population. At the same time the world's population is growing at a rate of .88%. (073)

Although Christians comprise just under a third of the world's people, they form a majority of the population in 158 countries and territories, about two-thirds of all the countries and territories in the world. (074)

If the Lord delays His coming, according to a 2015 Pew Research Centre study, the Christian population globally is expected to be 3 billion by 2050. (075) The Enemy hates the thought of that, so he's doing all he can to destroy the church by working through the media, corrupt governments, despots, dictators and globalists to stir up persecution against it. But, he will never reverse the growth and influence of the church, because Jesus said, *Matthew 16:18 "I will build my church, and all the powers of hell will not conquer it."* NLT

The church is rising and shining in this generation like never before in history. We are beginning to see in this generation the harvest Jesus spoke of that would indicate the end of the age and His return to this planet. This great harvest of humanity could have been happening hundreds of years ago but it's happening now in this generation. I believe we're living in the most exciting time in history. All around us we are seeing the signs Jesus was giving regarding the nearness of His coming. He is right at the door.

- Israel has returned to Palestine.
- Israel is prospering, the fig tree is blossoming.
- Deception and lies are infiltrating every aspect of life.
- Fear has become a global virus.
- The One World Government is forming.
- The False Prophet is speaking.
- The Days of Noah are here again with Hybrid Humans.
- The Mark of the Beast is ready to enslave all.
- International Alliances opposed to Israel are forming.
- World travel is increasing.
- Exponential growth in knowledge is here.
- Persecution of Believers is on the increase.
- The Gospel is reaching the four corners of the earth.
- The Church is Rising.

All of these events/signs could have been spread out as stand-alone and separate events over hundreds of years into the past or yet to unfold sometime in the distant future, but they're all coming together in this generation.

The Apostle Peter in his second letter asks a question that is extremely relevant for those living at the time of Jesus return. We find it in...

Chapter 3:9-11 The Lord is not slow about His promise, as some count slowness, but is patient toward you, not wishing for any to perish but for all to come to repentance. But the day of the Lord will come like a thief, in which the heavens will pass away with a roar and the elements will be destroyed with intense heat, and the earth and its works will be burned up. Since all these things are to be destroyed in this way, what sort of people ought you to be in holy conduct and godliness, looking for and hastening the coming of the day of God... NLT

What a great question to be asking of this generation. What sort of people ought we to be? The answer is simple. We ought to be people who've committed our lives to Jesus Christ, making Him our Lord and Saviour. We ought to be people putting our hope and trust in the Lord. We ought to be committed to a local Bible believing church where we can grow in our understanding of God and His ways. We ought to be people who are living our lives in a way that is pleasing to Him. We ought to be people exposing the evils being perpetrated in the world. As the world grows darker we ought to be people sharing our faith with others, and declaring that the coming of the Lord is near. We ought to be people who are continually anticipating the return of our Lord Jesus Christ

I hope and pray that by reading through the pages of this book you will be inspired to do just that. In Jesus Name.

APPENDIX

001 - *Acts 1:11, Acts 3:19-21, 1 Cor 1:7, 1 Cor 4:5, 1 Cor 11:26, 1 Cor 15:23-24, Col 3:4, 1 Thess 1:10, 1 Thess 2:19, 1 Thess 3:13, 1 Thess 4:15-16 1 Thess 5:23, 2 Thess 1:7, 2 Thess 2:1, 2 Thess 2:8, 1 Tim 6:14, Titus 2:12-14, Heb 9:28, James 5:7, 1 Pet 1:13, 1 Pet 5:14, 2 Pet 1:16, 1 John 2:28, Rev 1:7-8,*

002 - Bounfour, Ahmed; Edvinsson, Leif (2005). *Intellectual Capital for Communities: Nations, Regions, and Cities.* Butterworth-Heinemann. p. 47 (368 pages).

003 - Richard Behar (11 May 2016). "Inside Israel's Secret Startup Machine". *Forbes.* Retrieved 30 October 2016.

004 - Human Development Report 2021-22: Uncertain Times, Unsettled Lives: Shaping our Future in a Transforming World (PDF). hdr.undp.org. United Nations Development Programme. 8 September 2022. pp. 272–276.

005 - "Global Wealth Databook 2022" (PDF). Credit Suisse. Archived (PDF) *from the original on 19 October 2022.* Retrieved 19 October *2022.* Financial assets by adult in selected countries on page 109.

006 - "Israel Economic Snapshot – OECD". *www.oecd. org.* Retrieved 10 February 2023.

007 – https://dreddymd.com/2020/10/09/who-tangled-up-in-big-pharmas-web-of-influence/

008 – TV morning show "Sunrise" 20th May 2023

009 – https://nypost.com/2023/05/23/pandemic-even-deadlier-than-covid-is-coming-warns-who/

010 – https://odysee.com/@TruthPills:5/The-Fear-Pandemic:e

011 -- https://concernedamericandad.com/2021/12/07/dr-mark-mcdonald-covid-the-united-states-of-fear-a-psychiatric-perspective-on-vaccination-mandates-authoritarianism/

012 – https://www.weforum.org/agenda/2022/12/the-20-humanitarian-crises-the-world-cannot-ignore-in-2023-and-what-to-do-about-them/

013 – https://humansbefree.com/2016/01/henry-kissinger-top-architect-of-the-new-world-order.html

014 – https://www.telesurenglish.net/news/Guterres-Proposes-Emergency-Platform-to-Tackle-Global-Shocks-20230310-0004.html

015 – https://www.wnd.com/2022/03/world-government-summit-ready-new-world-order/

016 – https://ac.news/the-death-of-freedom-un-unleashing-digital-army-to-censor-online-disinformation-all-around-the-world/

017 -- https://en.wikipedia.org/wiki/New_World_Order_(conspiracy_theory)

018 – https://nsarchive.gwu.edu/document/29753-document-1-memorandum-secretary-state-designate-warren-christopher-lawrence-s

019 – https://thenewamerican.com/us/politics/kissinger-urges-obama-to-build-a-new-world-order/

020 – https://www.rt.com/news/341302-global-order-cooperation-rudd/

021 – https://cdn.preterhuman.net/texts/conspiracy/New World_Order/NWO.-.Final.Warning.-.History. of.the.New.World.Order.pdf

022 – https://the-complete-truth.blogspot.com/p/new-world-order-quotes-its-planned-its.html

023 -- https://the-complete-truth.blogspot.com/p/new-world-order-quotes-its-planned-its.html

024 -- https://www.youtube.com/watch?v=72niWJWYROo

025 – https://the-complete-truth.blogspot.com/p/new-world-order-quotes-its-planned-its.html

026 – https://the-complete-truth.blogspot.com/p/new-world-order-quotes-its-planned-its.html

027 – https://the-complete-truth.blogspot.com/p/new-world-order-quotes-its-planned-its.html

028 – https://the-complete-truth.blogspot.com/p/new-world-order-quotes-its-planned-its.html

029 – https://yandex.com/video/preview/8412538409226160897

030 – https://www.rt.com/news/552434-biden-new-world-order/

031 -- https://www.youtube.com/watch?v=hzpzA8W479k

032 -- https://www.youtube.com/watch?v=8MXXU_zuU6w

033 – https://the-complete-truth.blogspot.com/p/new-world-order-quotes-its-planned-its.html

034 – https://the-complete-truth.blogspot.com/p/new-world-order-quotes-its-planned-its.html

035 -- https://humansbefree.com/2021/11/world-leaders-serve-the-new-world-order.html

036 – https://discoveringmybeliefs.wordpress.com/nwo/

037 – https://www.azquotes.com/author/5626-Joseph_ Goebbels

038 -- https://www.naturalnews.com/2022-02-09-covid-vaccines-make-hackable-humans-a-reality.html https:// yandex.com/video/preview/10681015521284591587

039 – NineNews.com.au 16th September 2023

040 – whitehouse.gov 24th May 2023

041 – https://medium.com/@sughranawaz45/shanghai-cooperation-organization-sco-7da2afbf01cb

042 – https://military-history.fandom.com/wiki/List_of_ wars_by_death_toll

043 – https://nypost.com/2023/08/18/ukraine-war-troop-deaths-injuries-near-500k-officials/

044 -- https://www.abs.gov.au/statistics/industry/tourism-and-transport/motor-vehicle-census-australia/ latest-release

045 -- https://theconversation.com/overcrowded-trains-serve-as-metaphor-for-india-in-western-eyes-but-they-are-a-relic-of-colonialism-and-capitalism-207169

046 – https://financesonline.com/number-of-flights-worldwide/

International Civil Aviation Organization https://www. icao.int › annual-report-2019 › Pages › the-...

047 – https://www.cruisemummy.co.uk/cruise-industry-statistics-facts/

048 – https://www.mindset.solutions/post/the-knowledge -doubling-curve

049 – https://www.bbc.com/news/world-europe-60111140

050 – https://www.theblaze.com/news/canadian-pastor -artur-pawlowski-arrested

051 – https://nypost.com/2023/03/16/pastor-derek-reimer-arrested-again-for-drag-queen-storytime-protest/

052 – https://www.wnd.com/2021/05/shocking-video-christian-pastor-frogmarched-preaching-bible/

053 – https://nypost.com/2022/07/09/christian-americans-are-sick-of-being-punished-for-their-views/

054 – https://religionnews.com/2022/09/19/are-american-christians-on-the-path-to-severe-persecution-for-their-faith/

055 – https://wng.org/opinions/australian-territory-attacks-faith-1691554178

056 – https://wng.org/opinions/australian-territory-attacks-faith-1691554178

057 – https://www.dailymail.co.uk/news/article-11056519/Bob-Katter-claims-Christianity-attack-Australia-Manly-Sea-Eagles-jersey-fiasco.html

058 – https://www.newsbusters.org/blogs/free-speech/luis-cornelio/2023/05/25/how-bidens-dhs-weaponizing-anti-terror-program-against

059 – https://www.opendoors.org/en-US/persecution/countries/

060 – https://www.churchinneed.org/christian-persecution/

061 – https://www.pewforum.org/wp-content/uploads/sites/7/2019/07/Restrictions_X_WEB_7-15_FULL-VERSION-1.pdf

062 -- https://nebraskasynod.org/wp-content/uploads/2021/08/WesGM-NES_speaker1.pdf

063 -- https://nebraskasynod.org/wp-content/uploads/2021/08/WesGM-NES_speaker1.pdf

064 – https://www.cfan.eu/the-mission-organisation-of-reinhard-bonnke-and-daniel-kolenda/

065 – https://www.christianity.com/wiki/cults-and-other-religions/why-are-thousands-of-muslims-converting-to-christ.html

066 – https://www.thegospelcoalition.org/article/meet-the-worlds-fastest-growing-evangelical-movement/

067 – https://www.theechonews.com/article/2022/04/korean-christianity-sets-example

068 – https://www.pewresearch.org/religion/2013/07/18/brazils-changing-religious-landscape/

069 – https://www.dw.com/en/how-pentecostal-churches-are-changing-brazil/a-63283164

070 – https://www.asiaharvest.org/christians-in-china-stats

071 – https://www.joyfulheart.com/misc/growth-of-christianity-in-india.htm

072 – https://www.bbc.com/news/world-asia-64235873

073 – https://www.gordonconwell.edu/center-for-global-christianity/wp-content/uploads/sites/13/2022/01/Status-of-Global-Christianity-2022.pdf

074 – https://www.pewresearch.org/religion/2011/12/19/global-christianity-exec/#:~:text=Although%20Christians%20comprise%20just%20under,and%20territories%20in%20the%20world.

075 – https://www.pewresearch.org/religion/2015/04/02/christians/

Printed in the United States
by Baker & Taylor Publisher Services